REVELATION
AS HISTORY

REVELATION AS HISTORY

EDITED BY
Wolfhart Pannenberg

IN ASSOCIATION WITH
Rolf Rendtorff, Trutz Rendtorff, & Ulrich Wilkens

TRANSLATED FROM THE GERMAN BY
David Granskou

The Macmillan Company
Collier-Macmillan Ltd · London

Library of Congress Catalog Card Number: 67-20185

First Macmillan Paperbacks Edition 1969

Revelation As History is published in a hardcover edition
by The Macmillan Company

The original edition of this book was published in Germany in 1961
under the title *Offenbarung Als Geschichte* by Vandenhoeck & Ruprecht,
Göttingen

The Macmillan Company
Collier-Macmillan Canada Ltd., Toronto, Ontario

PRINTED IN THE UNITED STATES OF AMERICA

CONTENTS

FOREWORD

The studies in this book were first presented at a theological workshop in October 1960, and although slightly modified, they retain the provisional form of such presentations. These papers emerge from a cross-fertilization of systematic and historical disciplines and in this way have a common statement of the problem. The introductory lecture sketches out the overarching theme, which is then taken up and tested exegetically.

The two biblical treatments proceed in methodologically distinct ways. The Old Testament lecture is more oriented to a conceptual approach that would still call for a traditio-historical supplementation, while the New Testament lecture presents a traditio-historical sketch of the primitive Christian understanding of revelation with less emphasis on a conceptual approach and investigation into the different terms for "revelation." A balanced lecture would have to utilize the two methods in concert, for they complement each other. The casting of the systematic lecture in the form of theses would acknowledge that not all the problems that have relevance for the theme could be dealt with in such a form. The concluding lecture is an appraisal of the connection between the concept of the church and the problem of revelation.

WOLFHART PANNENBERG

PREFACE TO THE AMERICAN EDITION

This book was the outcome of a combined effort of a group of young German theologians to bridge the gulf between exegesis and systematic theology. On the basis of exegetical investigations, following a brief historical introduction (concerned with the modern history of the concept of revelation), a reinterpretation of this key concept of modern theology is proposed: Revelation is no longer understood in terms of a supernatural disclosure or of a peculiarly religious experience and religious subjectivity, but in terms of the comprehensive whole of reality, which, however, is not simply given, but is a temporal process of a history that is not yet completed, but open to a future, which is anticipated in the teaching and personal history of Jesus. To speak of revelation in this way does not involve any irreducible claims to authority, but is open to rational discussion and investigation.

This reinterpretation of the idea of revelation is directed against both the Barthian and the Bultmannian understanding of the word of God as the basis of theology. Without devoting itself to much explicit criticism of these positions, the book silently breaks with the basic presupposition that these two types of neo-orthodox theology have in common, with their authoritarian attitude, expressed in their idea of the divine Word and of the obedience it calls for. The idea of the Word is not excluded, but restituted to a more modest and subordinate role within the context of revelation as history. Instead of the authoritarian style of theological thought, the open rationality of the Enlightenment is preferred, but combined with a concern for the substance of the Christian tradition.

The appearance of the book in Germany in 1961 was followed by years of vivid discussion of the issues in various theological journals. The book received the theological basis which it had questioned. An answer to this criticism can be found in the second German edition, 1963 (postscript), and, more recently, in *Theology as History*, eds. James Robinson and John Cobb (*New Frontiers in Theology*, vol. 3, 1967).

I

Introduction

Wolfhart Pannenberg

Contemporary protestant theology has been quick to characterize itself as a pure theology of revelation. This is especially evident in Karl Barth and in the wide sphere of his influence. His theology has been walled off against any mixture of "natural," nontheological, and non-Christian knowledge. Only what can be founded on the revelation in Christ is valid as a dogmatic statement. In the background is Albrecht Ritschl's struggle for the uniqueness of revelation in Christ opposed to all conceptions of God in Greek metaphysics. Ritschl's antipathy against natural theology is taken to the extreme by Barth. While others from "dialectical theology" have not followed Barth in this emphasis and insist on the necessity of a point of contact with "natural" man, they also would like to be known as theologians concerned to have a theology based on revelation. Older theologies, like that of biblical *Heilsgeschichte* and the Erlangen neo-Lutheranism, had such a starting point in the concept of revelation; Barth has picked this up with less inhibition and greater self-understanding. Today, the term "revelation" has lost its value in theological usage. As long ago as 1941, Paul Althaus spoke of an "inflation" of this term.[1]

1. Revelation as Self-Revelation

If we study contemporary dogmatics for the meaning of the concept "revelation," we find a confusing variety of meaning. Some theologians speak of manifestation and inspiration, of revelation as act and as word, of primal revelation and revelation of salvation; others find revelations not only in God's history with Israel, but also in nature as the underlying phenomenon

3

of all religious experience; still others allow for only the one
revelation of God in the person of Jesus Christ. Yet, over and
above all of these distinctions is the present consensus that
revelation is, in essence, the self-revelation of God.[2]

Revelation is not God's making known a certain set of arcane
truths, but—as Karl Barth puts it—the self-disclosure of God.[3]
From its beginnings, Christian theology was aware that in every
revelation God's prime disclosure is of himself. The new stress
is the exclusive use of the concept "revelation" to mean the
self-disclosure of God, without any imparting of supernatural
truths. This innovation can be classed as a legacy of German
idealism. The Enlightenment destroyed the old concept of
revelation that belonged to seventeenth-century orthodox
dogmatics, namely, the identification of revelation and the
inspiration of Holy Scripture, the understanding of revelation
as the transmission of supernatural and hidden truths. The
assertion of such a revelation was suspected of fostering an
obscurantism that would avoid the light of scientific reason.
From the beginning of the nineteenth century, there was the
suspicion that supernaturalism is superstition, and the concept
of revelation could only be rescued by means of reducing its
content to God's *self*-revelation. This reduction amounts to
a definition excluding everything purely miraculous. Whereas
as late as 1816 the supernaturalist Tittmann was still maintaining the old idea of an unmediated, revealed set of facts and
doctrine alongside his definition of revelation as a "manifestation or activity in time whereby the divine is made known to
man," Schleiermacher chose to limit the concept of revelation
to the religious sphere.[4] However, like the young Schelling,
Schleiermacher still thought of a multiplicity of self-manifesta-
tions by God, about a variety of insights into the universe,
which are, however, not distinct in principle.

The strictly defined concept of revelation as the self-revelation
of the absolute appears to have been first introduced by Hegel,
for with him it became clear for the first time that the full self-

manifestation of God can only be a unique one. Hegel expressly reserved the designation "a revealed and revealing religion" for Christianity, not because it contains truths that have been transmitted by supernatural means, but because, in distinction from all other religions, it rests on full disclosure of the nature of the absolute as spirit.[5]

Self-revelation is thus so strictly understood that it is no longer permissible to think of a medium of revelation that is distinct from God himself. Or rather: The creaturely medium of revelation, the man Jesus Christ, is caught up to God in his distinctiveness and received in unity with God himself. A means of revelation that in itself remains creaturely and holds to its distinctiveness from God would of course imply a sort of pollution of the divine light, presuppose an inadequate manifestation, and prevent the development of a full revelation. As the Hegelian Philipp Marheineke said: "It is not through the human spirit as such that God is revealed, but through himself and then to the human spirit."[6] It is out of the question that the human spirit as such would be able to see God himself! Marheineke's sentence is echoed in Karl Barth's thesis that God's revelation to man cannot be apprehended by his own power, but only by means of God through the Holy Spirit. Actually, Barth has repeatedly cited Marheineke's sentence, and in respect to his concept of revelation he has heaped an extraordinary amount of praise on him.[7]

Barth's understanding of revelation has other roots as well, but its exclusive conception as the self-revelation of God would have its source here. This is corroborated in Barth's doctrine of the Trinity understood as the development of the concept of revelation, and here Barth's *Church Dogmatics* follows Hegel's philosophy of religion.[8] The fairness of this comparison will become clear in the course of the subsequent exegetical and dogmatic investigations. We should also remember that to locate a theological thought in German idealism is not automatically to condemn it.

Barth's strict conception of God's self-disclosure issues in a novel stress on the *uniqueness of revelation*. Those rejecting Barth's conception that revelation in Christ is the truly unique one have obviously not properly considered that the uniqueness of revelation is already implied in the context of "self-revelation." If God is already totally revealed in the special decisiveness of the Christ event, than he cannot in consistency be "also" revealed in other events, situations, and persons. Speaking of many revelations is no longer thinking of revelation in the strictest sense. A multiplicity of revelation implies a discrediting of any particular revelation, for then the form of the divine manifestation is no longer the singularly adequate expression of the revealer. God may be more or less transparent in any of these forms, but in none of them is he revealed in a full and exclusive sense. In actuality, the theologians who speak of a variety of revelations do not take the concept in the strict sense that Barth does. They speak of his manifestations through diverse means that emanate from him, or by indirect manifestation in activities that originate in him. But while the creaturely media through which God is perceptible do manifest him, and while the activities that emanate from him do refer back to their originator, they are still diverse. In either case, there are many "revelations."

The first possibility, namely, the direct transparence of divine power through a medium that is distinct from God, approximates to the usage employed in the study of religion. This usage, which has roots in the thought of Schelling, is to be found in Troeltsch and Tillich as well as in van der Leeuw.[9]

The second possibility, namely, the indirect self-authentication of God on the basis of his activity, can be found in the distinction Paul Althaus and Emil Brunner make between revelation in creation and revelation of salvation on the basis of the economy of salvation; but there is no explicit distinction between this possibility and the first, and in Brunner the two in practice amount to the same thing.[10]

Both of these ways of looking at revelation lead to the establishment of essential theological content and are not simply misleading: the biblical witnesses report epiphanies of God, more or less veiled in mystery, veiled because of the creaturely medium through which they occur. More important for the problem of revelation is the indirect self-authentication of God through his acts. We will have to go into this more carefully later. But first, according to the biblical witnesses, it is not a matter of two acts of God, but of an incalculable fullness. And second, no single act of God can cause its originator to be known completely, precisely because it is only one act among many. In either case, the problem of revelation in the strictest sense of God's self-disclosure has not yet come into view. One can think of revelation in the strict sense only if the special means by which God becomes manifest, or the particular act by which he proves himself, is not seen as distinct from his own essence. Karl Barth recognized this before any of the theologians of his day by stressing the unity of God with Jesus Christ in the context of his conception of revelation.[11] The unity of Jesus with God is a unity-in-revelation and as such implies a unity of essence. The unity Jesus has with God in revelation must therefore be the root of christological statements about the divinity of Jesus Christ.[12]

In an extension of the Barthian point of departure by Heinrich Vogel, it is stated that the uniqueness of revelation follows from the strict concept of self-revelation.[13] In Barth, himself, this fundamental insight is partly endangered by the assertion that the "form" of revelation also implies a veiling.[14]

If, however, the revelation is truly revelation so that its special form belongs totally to itself, then this form cannot, at the same time, be a veiling. Here it is as if Barth's presentation follows the dialectic of the philosophy of religion and takes over where the means of revelation seem to mediate both veiled and transparent appearances of the deity. The conception of a God who by nature has a veiled form of manifestation (the veiling is not just against those who misunderstand) runs contrary to the unity of revelation as the self-revelation: It could yield just

as many divine manifestations as veiled forms. However, this
would lose the fundamental insight of Barth into the essence of
revelation as self-revelation. Only if the form of revelation
reveals God and—rightly understood—does not veil him, only
then is Barth's thesis of the unity of revelation tenable.

2. The Problem of a Biblical Validation of the Thought of God's Self-Revelation

These reflections so far have merely established the fact of the
general dispersion in the contemporary theology of the idea
regarding the self-revelation of God, as well as the connection of
the unity of revelation with the formal structure of the concept
"self-revelation." It is in no way obvious how the theological
utilization of this concept is to be justified and just how the
self-revelation of God is to be concretely explicated. This
question could be answered in a variety of ways. The varieties
of solutions reflect the deep-seated difficulties in the problem
itself.

The question of the self-revelation of God must somehow be
confirmed on the basis of the biblical witnesses if it is to be
theologically justifiable. This assertion is not just protestant bias,
but accords with the recognition of the biblical scriptures as the
fundamental witnesses of the events to which theology relates
when it speaks of revelation. However, at first glance, there is no
terminological usage concerning the self-revelation of God in the
biblical writings. This is particularly true in the New Testament.
The Greek terms rendered by "to reveal" do not in any passage
of the New Testament have God as an unqualified object.[15]
God continually reveals "something" or "someone," never
precisely "himself." Such a formulation is to be found for the
first time in Ignatius (Magn. 8:2). An investigation of the
Hebrew terms that are rendered "to reveal" does not result in
anything essentially different. The Old Testament essay will
demonstrate this with more precision.

The oldest Israelitic traditions report appearances of Jahweh that led to a foundation of a cultic place or introduced certain important information. But the one who appeared did not in any way reveal his essence. I would like to designate such appearances henceforth not as revelation, as is unfortunately the practice in the study of religion, but as "manifestations." By "manifestations" I mean any appearance of God that does not involve the disclosure of essence. Self-revelation (*revelation: unveiling*) as the disclosure of essence is distinguished from a purely phenomenal understanding of manifestation. The appearances of Jahweh, which the Old Testament report from time to time, ought not to be rendered "to reveal himself." Quite apart from such appearances, the terminological investigation of equivalent terms for "to reveal" does not lead, even in the Old Testament, to a simple or obvious solution concerning the question of the self-revelation of God. This is especially true of the many visions, including the reception of the word in the prophets, that are reported in this terminology. Here, Jahweh always imparted "something" specific, never simply himself.

We have shown that neither the Old nor New Testaments know of any terminological expression for the "self-revelation of God." Perhaps at this stage we ought to take the investigation beyond the limits of terminology. Next, I would like to consider some instances in which one can attempt to find the fact of a direct self-disclosure of God.

1. God's announcement of his name has been thought of by some to be a direct self-revelation. Thus Karl Barth (*Ch. Dog.*, I/1, pp. 363ff.) and Heinrich Vogel (*loc. cit.*, pp. 162ff.) in this respect. This interpretation seems plausible, because to ancient man the name is nothing purely outward, and the essence itself lives in the name of a person or thing. The impartation of the name, then, appears to signify that the essence itself has been made accessible. But the significance of the name-giving in Exodus 3 is not that henceforth the essence of God will be fully known to the Israelites. As 3:15 expressly states, the imparta-

tion of Jahweh's name is made so that man can appeal to God
by means of this name. This is a significant event—Israel thus
realizes the possibility of an association with Jahweh! But this is
not self-revelation in the sense of a full self-disclosure. In this
respect, it is noteworthy that Jahweh's answer to Moses'
concern about his name did, in effect, dodge the question (so
Grether, v. Rad). And this occurs in the priestly version of this
tradition where the declaration of the name is most radically
stylized as a marvelous disclosure (Ex. 6) and is immediately
followed by a reference to knowledge of Jahweh only to be had
in the future (6:7). The giving of the name in such a passage
can hardly be classed as an example of full self-revelation.

Therefore, if the Old Testament tradition of the proclamation of the name of Jahweh does not contain the concept of a
complete self-disclosure of God, then one cannot go along with
Barth and Vogel and by analogy view the name Jesus Christ
as the essence of New Testament revelation. There is no reason
to contest the decisive meaning of this name for the Christian
faith, but here, also, the simple knowledge of the name does not
imply a full understanding of the being involved in the name.
This would be the case if the name functioned as a self-revelation.

2. Likewise, in the history of the biblical tradition, "the
Word of God" does not have, or is only on the verge of having,
the meaning that modern personalistic theology invests in it.[16]
In the traditions of Israel, as in those of primitive Christianity,
the term "the Word of God" is used in a variety of meanings.
The final essay will come back to this. But first of all, one thing
should be stressed: While the word authorized by Jahweh or
spoken by him had fundamental meaning in the thought of
Israel, it still had, in all its manifold functions, concrete contents that are distinct from God. It never had God as its content in any unmediated way. This was also true of the creative
Word of God that was not mediated through men. The same is
true for the bulk of primitive Christian tradition. One may study
the question of the Word of God in Paul, deutero-Pauline

material, the synoptics, or especially in the Lucan complex, Luke–Acts. When the author speaks of the Word of God, he has in mind the apostolic kerygma. Here, too, is an entity whose content is clearly distinct from God himself.

The term "the Word of God" also designates the commands of God and the prophetic word in the mouth of Jesus and in the eschatological congregation. Finally, in the Book of Revelation, the Word of God and witness of Jesus (1:2f., 9), also the witness of Jesus and the spirit of the prophets (19:10f.; cf. 19:13), are closely linked together. The conception of a direct self-disclosure of God in the Word, even if mediated by a proclaimer, is to be found in the New Testament only to the extent that gnostic concepts of revelation become clearly manifest. In Hebrews 1:2 (cf. 2:2f.), the formulations of the eschatological speeches of God in the Son come close to a direct revelation of the Word, and more especially, the Logos in John 1:1ff., although here, as in the Odes of Solomon 12 and 16, the Logos is primarily a cosmological entity and only as such has a function in revelation. The Johannine Logos is still distinct from the expression of Ignatius (Magn. 8:2) that Christ would be the Word by which God broke his silence.

With respect to the conception of revelation in the prologue and Gospel of John, and perhaps also Col. 1:25ff., one could argue that the gnostic concept of revelation has been broken by its connection with the tradition of Jesus, because its connection with this tradition gave it an element of indirectness totally foreign to gnosticism.

In any event, if we want to match up the particular characteristics of this many-sided conception in Israelitic and primitive Christian thought with the dogmatic concept Word of God, then we ought not to proceed from formulations that bear the strong stamp of the gnostic understanding of revelation, nor from the understanding of the unmediated creative Word which Israel has in common with the ancient Orient. If we do not wish to lose the specifically biblical content, then we must

first of all orient the dogmatic concept of the Word of God
to the words of God connected with the history of Israel and
primitive Christianity—words that have various functions and
specific content. Consequently, we will not venture to take the
personalistic concept of the Word as a basic from the outset,
because this does not really take account of the declarative
character and consequently the concrete contents and particular function in which the specific character of the biblical
understanding of the Word first become visible. The modern
personalistic theology of the Word (influenced by Ferdinand
Ebner, Martin Buber, and others), where Word is primarily
the direct engagement of a person to a Thou, has its closest
parallel not in the specifically biblical context, but rather in the
gnostic understanding of the Word. This is apparent in the
formulation of Ignatius, which can hardly be found in an un-
reconstructed state within the New Testament, or at least
only on the periphery. Only in gnostic thought does Word
appear as the bearer of a direct divine self-revelation. The real
problem is the extent to which we may deviate from the biblical
understanding of revelation in the use of a gnostic understanding of revelation and a gnostic concept of the Word. This problem will still be our concern in the final lecture. Now it suffices
to insist that if one wishes to understand specifically biblical
functions and contents, then the Word of God does not have the
character of a direct self-revelation of God.

3. Thus the proclamation of the *Law* on Sinai is not to be
understood as a direct self-revelation of Jahweh, namely, a
disclosure of the essence of his will which would then be matched
as revelation with the New Testament proclamation of the
gospel. Werner Elert[17] has attempted to understand Law and
gospel as the two dialectically opposed aspects of the biblical
revelation of God, that is, to substitute the dialectic of Law and
gospel for the problem of revelation. Rendtorff will demonstrate
in the following essay that Law as an entity by itself is not
revelation, but rather followed from revelation. The authority

of the Law is grounded in the authority of Jahweh, which is presupposed as known and proved in a different way (Ex. 20:2; Lev. 19:1ff.). Likewise, we must not assume the gospel stems from a revelation that was spoken; rather it refers to one that has happened. To make such an assumption is already to link the salvation proclaimed in the gospel with the concept of a self-revelation of God. This correction is what is suspect.

Thus, while the distinction between Law and gospel is of fundamental importance for theology, it ought not be taken as a twofold, direct, self-revelation of God. No theology of revelation can in any direct way take its point of departure from here.

Finally, it must be concluded that the theological assertion of a direct self-revelation of God cannot be justified either on the basis of the biblical equivalents for "to reveal" or on the basis of the three aforesaid areas of conception, to which such a meaning has been ascribed. Even if other concepts such as the glory of God did originally contain the implication of a direct self-revelation, they have been absorbed in the Old Testament tradition by the point of view that is decisive for Israel, namely, the fundamental proof for the divinity of Jahweh exists in his acts in history. Instead of a direct self-revelation of God, the facts at this point indicate a conception of indirect self-revelation as a reflex of his activity in history. The totality of his speech and activity, the history brought about by God, shows who he is in an indirect way. The negative statements on the lack of or the suppression of the concept of a direct self-revelation of God are first felt with full weight in connection with the meaning that this indirect self-revelation of God has in the whole of Israelitic, apocalyptic, and primitive Christian history of tradition.

3. The Problems Involved in an Indirect Self-Revelation of God Through History

In the previous investigation we rejected the conception of a direct self-revelation of God through his name, his Word, or through Law and gospel. What has finally emerged in contrast is the thought of an indirect self-revelation of God as a reflex of his activity in history. The exegetical investigations of the two following essays will demonstrate that this thought corresponds to the Israelite and primitive Christian testimonies of faith; that (and how) it comes to expression in them; and how far it shaped the tenor of the biblical history of tradition. But first, I propose to occupy myself with a somewhat more precise terminological distinction between direct and indirect revelation. Toward this end, I shall go into the relationship between direct and indirect communication.

Direct communication has in an immediate way just that content that it intends to communicate, whereas indirect communication initially has some other content than that which is actually to be communicated. Direct communication transmits content without a break from the sender to the receiver. In indirect communication, the path is broken: the content first reveals its actual meaning by being considered from another perspective. Indirect communication is on a higher level: it always has direct communication as its basis, but takes this into a new perspective.

Whether the communication is transmitted by means of a third party or is directly delivered to the recipient is inconsequential for the distinction between direct and indirect communication. As is well known, protestant orthodoxy spoke of an unmediated revelation that was imparted to the prophets and apostles through inspiration and distinguished this from a mediated revelation, because all who lived later participated in revelation only by mediation of the prophetic and apostolic witness. (At this stage revelation was not yet reduced to the concept of self-revelation.) However, direct communication does not necessarily require immediateness, for it can also require a messenger. In any event, the theories of inspiration had in mind a direct communication. Vice versa, the indirect communication can very easily be unmediated and received without a middleman. The distinction between direct and indirect communication is not therefore dependent on whether the communication requires a mediator or not. It is not a question of mediateness or immediateness in the *act* of communication, but whether the content.of a communication can be linked in a direct or indirect way with its intention.

Thus, direct communication would have God himself—without mediation—as its content, analogous to divine epiphanies in the sense of a complete self-revelation, and communication of the divine name would be a direct revelation if it involved a direct disclosure of the being of God himself. The Law would be direct revelation if it were identical with God's will, which is itself the essence of God. The Word of God would be direct communication if its content were directly connected with God himself, somewhat in the sense of a self-presentation of the divinity. Symbolic self-communication stands on the border between direct and indirect communication. When a symbol is supposed to have a divine content, it is direct revelation to the extent that it suppresses its own primary and unsymbolic meaning in favor of its symbolism. In this sense, gnostic revelation is direct, even though the divine spirit is communicated in symbolic form.

Indirect communication is distinguished by not having God as the content in any direct manner. Every activity and act of God can indirectly express something about God. It can say that God is the one who does this or that. Here the event in question does not have the same aspect as it would if one merely stood under the impact of its content. Not only is the content perceived for its own value; it is also seen that the event defined in this way has God as its originator. Here lies the change of perspective. Though the primary content of the event is still presupposed, there is simply a reflection on the event first perceived, and the stimulus to this derives from the event itself, or from the Word fulfilled in it, announcing the event as the act of Jahweh. As acts of God, these acts cast light back on God himself, communicating something indirectly about God himself. That does not of course mean that they reveal God or that God reveals himself in them as their originator, for every individual event which is taken to be God's activity illuminates the being of God only in a partial way. God will carry out many things which cannot be foreseen, and they will also point back to their originator, though in different ways. Thus no one act could be a full revelation of God. The isolated conception of a single divine action as the revelation of God most often leads to a distorted view, to an idol.

If we wish to understand the indirect self-communication that resides in every individual act of God as revelation, then there are as many revelations as there are divine acts and occurrences in nature and history. But this destroys the strict sense of revelation as self-revelation of God. Only then is it possible to understand the totality of God's action—and if God is one then that means everything that happens—as his revelation. There are, therefore, two possibilities: If the totality of reality in its unalterable relationship (as cosmos) is understood as the indirect communication of the true God, then we are on the road of the Greek philosophical questions of God, that of "natural theology." In contrast, when the totality of reality in its temporal development is thought of as history and as the self-communication of God, then we find ourselves on the road which German idealism has taken since the time of Lessing and Herder.[18]

The express assertion that history as a totality is God's revelation and that this is the mark of Christianity in contrast to all other religions was enunciated in 1799 in Schleiermacher's fifth discourse on religion.[19]

A few years later (1802), Schelling stated these ideas as a formal principle in the ninth of his lectures on the method of academic study. Hegel gave systematic formulation to the conception of universal history as an indirect revelation of God in connection with his explication of the concept of self-revelation. The later Schelling further developed this aspect of Hegel.[20] They all wished to use this conception as validation of the biblical tradition and its way of thinking, but there are many serious objections that play against it not only from a philosophical, but also from a theological point of view. I shall limit myself to two points. First, if it is only in its totality that history is the revelation of God, how can a specific event within it, such as the fate of Jesus, have absolute meaning as revelation?

This is the question that Strauss raised against Hegel and Schleiermacher in his well-known statement at the close of his *Life of Jesus* (1835): that it is not the character of an idea to exhaust itself in its fullness in one particular individual instead of being presented in the development of its form. The idea that Strauss has in mind is the unity of God and man, which ought to hold true for the development of the human species rather than only in the one man, Jesus. As we have seen before (see note 6), since the God-man unity of the incarnation is closely linked with the Hegelian concept of the self-revelation of God, which constitutes its foundation, it is therefore significant for Strauss to dissolve the concept of revelation into his idea of the development of humanity.[21]

We could not demonstrate here just how far these thoughts of Strauss in no way represent a consistent result of the Hegelian development but are instead a fundamental misunderstanding of Hegel. This is only seldom recognized. One could confront Strauss dogmatically to the effect that the concept of revelation is not derived from an idea of the incarnation, but that the reverse is the case; the God-man unity in Jesus Christ is to be preserved by the fact of the revelation of God in him that is established in another way. Instead of this, not only Kierkegaard, but the whole theology that followed, reacted with a division, following the supranaturalist tradition, between the saving event and universal history.

Secondly, if history is to be the totality of revelation, then it appears that there is further progress that must be made beyond

Jesus Christ—about God's becoming manifest. In Hegel, this
departure was understood only as one of comprehending the
revelation that came about in Jesus. But it also appears necessary to reckon with a development in the facts themselves. The
effect of this question (which was much discussed in the period
after Hegel) on Kierkegaard is known.[22]

Not least because of this, the conception of Christianity
within the concept of universal history became an outrage to
him. The failure of the attempts to prove the absoluteness of
Christendom were already clear to see. Troeltsch needed only to
confirm these frustrations. Even until today, the belief in the
unsurpassability of Christianity appears to stand in tension
to the universal historical viewpoint. Connected with this is the
growing consciousness of all that happens being open to the
future. This is in opposition to Hegel and is motivated by an
emerging sense of the boundlessness and incomprehensibility of
history in its totality.

An essay by Richard Rothe has become particularly important for the development of the concept of revelation in the
second half of the nineteenth century.[23] The aftereffects of
German idealism are seen in Rothe in his conceiving of revelation as history, as a connection of events. For Rothe, scripture
describes the self-revelation of God as "a series of strange and
wonderful historical facts and events which have inner coher-
ence" (p. 59). He did this in contrast to the "inner miracle" of
the old traditional concept of inspiration, and to Schleiermacher's restrictive reconstruction of the doctrine of inspiration
on the basis of the inwardness of the pious consciousness. In
addition, Rothe no longer recognized the revelation of God in
history as a totality, but only in the "supernatural history" (p.
67) of the biblical tradition. These are the events that are "able
to clarify the idea of God only because they could not be logi-
cally derived from the world" (p. 66).

In this way, revelation was again limited to the sphere of
special biblical history, and like Hofmann's theory of *Heils-*

geschichte, Rothe was very seriously influenced by the old supernaturalism, although he himself carried out no division in principle between *Heilsgeschichte* (salvation history) and profane history. Above all, neither Rothe nor the champions of his very widely accepted thought of an outward "manifestation" of God in history have pursued just how a circumscribed series of outward events were not only God's activity by virtue of their source, but also beyond this would lead to the evidence of a full-blown self-revelation of God in them. Instead of this, Rothe as well as his followers, even including Ihmels and R. Seeberg, attempted a supplementation of the outward historical revelation by means of an inspiration whose meaning was revealed (so Rothe, Seeberg) or a "Word revelation."[24]

Such a supplement is unfortunate, however, because a revelation that requires supplementation to be manifest is not yet a true revelation. In those influenced by Rothe, there is still the unintentional hangover of an understanding of revelation in which inspiration is still the decisive and essentially revealing moment.[25] The idea of an indirect self-revelation of God through the history in which God is active is not new. It has its source in German idealism, as does the exclusive conception of revelation as self-revelation. Still, as I have indicated, it is burdened by a series of difficulties: an individual act of God, a particular event, can indeed cast an indirect light on its originator, but cannot be the full and complete revelation of the one God. However, history as a totality is not open to us as a self-contained unit. Still, if this were the case, it would not seem possible for any single event to have absolute meaning analogous to that of Jesus Christ in Christian faith, for universal history is simply too boundless and unremitting in its progress.

We wish to see whether the exegetical investigations in the Old and New Testaments serve as a basis for a conception of the indirect self-revelation of God which would be able to solve the above-mentioned difficulties.[26]

NOTES

1. *Zeitschrift für systematische Theologie*, vol. 18, 1941, pp. 134–49.
2. Thus in addition to Karl Barth there is also: Paul Althaus, *Die christliche Wahrheit*, 3rd ed., 1952, p. 21; E. Brunner, *The Christian Doctrine of God, Dogmatics*, vol. I, 1950, p. 14; H. Vogel, *Gott in Christo*, 1951, pp. 126f., 159 ff.; O. Weber, *Grundlagen der Dogmatik*, vol. I, 1955, pp. 184, 187 ff.; H. V. Oyen, *Theologische Erkenntnislehre*, 1955, p. 117; P. Tillich, *Systematic Theology*, vol. I, 1951, pp. 122f.; R. Bultmann, "The Concept of Revelation in the New Testament," in *Existence and Faith* (Meridian, S. Ogden, ed.), pp. 58ff.
3. K. Barth, *Church Dogmatics*, I/1, 1957, pp. 340ff.
4. F. Schleiermacher, *The Christian Faith*, # 10, Postscript.
5. F. Hegel, *The Phenomenology of the Mind*, vol. 2, 1961, pp. 695–96. According to Hegel, the unity of God and man, subject and object of revelation, is in Christ, God's revelatory essence (759). Cf. Schelling's eighth lecture on the method of academic study, 1803. Further: *Enzykl.* #564; philosophy of religion according to volume 15 of the jubilee edition of Hegel's works, p. 100, and vol. 16, pp. 192ff.
6. P. Marheineke, *Grundlehren der Dogmatik als Wissenschaft*, 1827, #115. In A. E. Biedermann it means something else, namely the "self authentication of God for man," in which the divine moment would be in the alternating relationship between the absolute and the finite spirit (*Christliche Dogmatik*, vol. II, 2nd ed., 1884, p. 264).
7. *Ch. Dog.*, I/1, pp. 279f.; *Die Prot. Theol. im 19. Jh.*, 2nd ed. 1948, p. 445.
8. Cf. *Ch. Dog.*, I/1, pp. 399ff., #8, p. 2; with Hegel's *Jubil.* ed., vol. 16, pp. 221f.
9. E. Troeltsch, *Die Absolutheit des Christentums*, 2nd ed., 1912, pp. 64, 75f., 103, and elsewhere; P. Tillich, "Die Idee der Offenbarung" *Z th K*, vol. 8, 1927; P. Tillich, *Systematic Theology*, vol. I, 1951, pp. 118, 159; G. van der Leeuw, *Religion in Essence and Manifestation* (Harper Torch book), #86.
10. P. Althaus, *Die Christliche Wahrheit*, #4–6; E. Brunner, *Dogmatics*, vol. I, pp. 14ff., 132ff.
11. *Ch. Dog.*, I/1, p. 340. "This God himself is not only himself but also his self-revelation" (343).
12. *Ch. Dog.*, I/1, p. 462. "The New Testament statement of the divinity of Christ means anything only as witnessing to God's revelation." Cf. pp. 474ff.
13. H. Vogel, *Gott in Christo*, 1951, p. 204.
14. *Ch. Dog.*, I/1, p. 369. It is noteworthy that in this train of thought Barth falls back on the Calvinistic axiom "finitum non capax infiniti" (pp. 73f.). Cf. also p. 199. However, this limitation is also the development of the supernatural understanding of revelation in which Barth thinks, and is to be understood in connection with the motifs of the theology of the cross and the concept of crisis in his *Commentary on Romans*.
15. H. Schulte, *Der Begriff der Offenbarung im Neuen Testament*, 1949, p. 42.
16. See Fr. Gogarten, *Der Mensch zwischen Gott und Welt*, 1952, pp. 234–74. Gogarten's statements constitute a particularly pure example of a personalistic theology of the Word whose distinctive characteristic is the disregard of the variety of the concrete contents and functions of the term "Word" in the biblical tradition. As is well known, this thought is widely disseminated in the contemporary kerygmatic theology.
17. Werner Elert, *Der Christliche Glaube*, 3rd ed., #23, pp. 138ff.

18. On this see D. W. Lütgert, *Die Religion des deutschen Idealismus und ihre Ende*, vol. I, 1923, pp. 153–85; and E. Fülling, *Geschichte als Offenbarung*, 1956.
19. *On Religion* (Harper Torchbook), pp. 210ff. Schleiermacher never developed this suggestion in any of his later writings.
20. W. Schulz, *Die Vollendung des deutschen Idealismus in der Spätphilosophie Schellings*, 1955, pp. 259–70.
21. D. F. Strauss, *Die Christliche Glaubenslehre*, I, 1840, pp. 274ff.
22. This shows itself in the ironic note on "to be continued" in the foreword and at the end of "Fear and Trembling," 1843.
23. R. Rothe, Revelation in: *Zur Dogmatik*, 1863, pp. 55ff. For earlier concerns in the same direction see R. Hermann, "Systematische bedeutsame Motive aus der Theologie des 19. Jh.," in *Dt. Ev. Theologentag*, 1960, ed. by W. Schneemelcher, pp. 17ff.; later, G. Gloege, *RGG*³, IV, 1610f.
24. R. Seeberg, *Offenbarung und Inspiration*, 1908; Ihmels, "Das Wesen der Offenbarung," in *Centralfragen der Dogmatik*, 1910, pp. 55–80, esp. 64ff.
25. J. Kaftan saw this correctly in *Das Wesen der Christliche Religion*, 2nd ed., 1888, pp. 322ff. (Cf. also Frank, *System der Christliche Gewissheit*, 1873, #47, note 14.) When Kaftan limits revelation to its manifestation in history in order to depend on its supplement in inspiration (*Dogmatik 1897*, 8th ed., 1920, #5, pp. 56f.), he finally comes to a conception similar to Rothe's since he views the outpouring of the spirit as an independent and indeed the decisive event of revelation (*Dogmatik*, #4, p. 47; *Wesen der Christl. Religion*, pp. 344ff.).
26. The judgment of G. Gloege, that the concept of the self-revelation of God "fails to account for the fragmentary character of revelation" (*RGG*, 3rd ed., IV, p. 1611), does, in my opinion, represent a very widespread understanding of this concept, while the indirectness that is stressed by Gloege has a fragmentary character. It is hardly possible to reject the concept of self-revelation, because it is constitutive for the thought of salvation as a fellowship with God (see p. 138), and because without it the theological use of the term "God" would lack its basis.

II

The Concept of Revelation in Ancient Israel

Rolf Rendtorff

At the present time, the term "revelation" has lost its value in theological usage.[1] This can be seen in recent presentations of Old Testament theology in which it can be encountered in many ways; the extent to which this discussion of revelation lacks unity is remarkable. Often a general concept of revelation is used, which is not well defined or grounded, notwithstanding the fact that this concept often ties together an entire presentation of Old Testament theology, or even serves as its basis. For example, in Eichrodt,[2] there is no section that expressly deals with "revelation," although the index lists some forty entries for "revelation" throughout this three-volume work. It is also striking to see how differently this concept can be developed even when it is thematically presented. In Procksch there is a section on "Revelation"[3] that stands at the head of the second main section, "The Thought World." Here we find a discussion on the "form of God" and the "Names of God." In Köhler, "the facts of revelation" (#19) are developed in a presentation of the concept "Covenant" (#20–23).[4] Jacob[5] begins his theology with a section "The Living God, Focal Point of Revelation and of Faith" (p. 37). He works out his understanding of revelation and also his whole theology of the Old Testament from the standpoint of a theologoumenon which, in the opinion of Köhler, can be found in the Old Testament "only occasionally, late and as a defense against the view that God has no life and no power."[6, 7]

In other cases, general and special concepts of revelation seem to develop alongside each other. Thus, later on in Köhler, there is a special section on "the revelation of God" (pp. 99ff.) in which various forms of revelation are treated, but no longer with a concern for the covenant. Also what is said in Procksch's section on revelation does not by any means cover the various ways he treats the concept within the total study. For instance, he employs the seemingly fundamental concept of prophet, as the bearer of revelation (pp. 215f.), and one who speaks of the Word of God as "an over-arching concept for revelation in general" (pp. 145f.). However, these isolated references have no recognizable connection with his special thematic treatment of revelation. And one can also find in his fundamental reflections the introduction of a still more inclusive concept of revelation that spans both Old Testament and New Testament. It is similar in Vriezen:[8] A fundamental section in the prolegomena deals with "the historical character of the revelation of God in Israel" (pp. 12ff.), in which, for example, there is discussion of "Old Testament witness as God's word of revelation" (p. 3, trans. from German text) or of an "on-going, teleological revelation of God" (p. 9, trans. from German text) in respect to the unity of the Old and New Testaments. Further on there is a special section on "the revelation of God" (pp. 233ff., trans. from German text), which deals with the "essence" and "forms" of revelation. While in Vriezen, the two do not exist without relationship to each other: The relation is accomplished by means of the speech about "the dealing of God with men" (p. 232 passim, trans. from German text), under which Vriezen groups the general and special understanding of revelation in the Old Testament. The question of just how the facts of revelation are spoken of in the Old Testament is relegated to the periphery of the discussion, and the "terms of revelation" are treated in four and a half lines without citations (p. 242).

There are obviously many reasons for this striking irregularity. On the one hand, the concept of revelation is such a self-evident element of contemporary theological language that one can use it without any special definition. Also, there seems to be little necessity to test these concepts of revelation by the Old

Testament expressions. On the other hand, there is difficulty in that the Old Testament does not possess any strictly formed concept of revelation. If we would pursue this question, several expressions present themselves; but no one of them can in itself be taken as the basis for an explication of the Old Testament understanding of revelation. Moreover, to this day we still are without a really usable investigation into the history of the concept; so that we must content ourselves with scattered studies on the varied terminology.[9] A responsible theological discourse of "revelation" would have to take its stand on Old and New Testament texts, and therefore an energetic inquiry into the Old Testament understanding of revelation is indispensable.

I

Although a clearly structured concept of revelation is lacking in the Old Testament, our investigation must begin by studying the terminology for revelation. The very structure of the Hebrew language would inhibit the development of nouns which could have embodied the concept "revelation."[10] Of the verbal roots relevant here, the LXX regularly renders גלה by ἀποκαλύπτειν, but an examination of the evidence demonstrates at once that the leading understanding of ἀποκαλύπτειν is not theological, but is "to expose, to unveil" in an everyday sense.[10a] This corresponds with the findings on גלה in which the nontechnical usage predominates. Where it does appear as a theological term, there is no unified understanding that undergirds it, so that it is unsuitable as a starting point for an investigation.[11]

1. As Pannenberg has shown in the previous essay, revelation in the strict sense is understood in current theological usage as the self-disclosure of God. In the Old Testament this content is never expressed in an unambiguous way and in a fixed theological terminology. Still, the Old Testament can speak in various ways of the self-manifestation or self-proclamation of Jahweh.

The most primitive and original usage occurs where it is said that the divinity "manifests himself." The niphal of ראה is the term expressing such appearances of God, and they are originally connected with a definite place. Thus, the place to which Moses came is precisely described in Exodus 3, which states "and the angel (*mal'āk*) of Jahweh appeared to him in a flame of fire out of the midst of a bush" (v. 2). This precise place, singled out by the appearance of the divine and thus honored, is the main thing; for this story in its original form was the etiology of a cultic place.[12]

This characteristic cultic-etiological usage of נראה has gone through a clearly perceptible history.

The Jahwist uses it repeatedly in an extremely condensed form. In the introductory section of the Abraham narrative, which was formulated by the Jahwist himself, it is said (Gen. 12:6f.) that Abraham came to the "oracle terebinth" ("the oak of Mareh"—RSV) in Shechem. "There the Lord appeared to Abram, and said, 'To your descendants I will give this land.' So he built there an altar to the Lord, who had appeared to him." The fundamental pattern of the cultic etiology can be perceived here: the deity appeared—and the man to whom this vision was given built an altar in response to it. The same pattern can be found in Gen. 26:24f., the appearance of Jahweh to Isaac at Beersheba. This is only the skeleton of a ἱερὸς λόγος without any narrative development. The Jahwist's own usages are strictly bound to tradition, as is demonstrated in his use of the pattern even when he is no longer interested in the local traditions themselves. Indeed, even in the priestly document the formal elements of this pattern can be encountered. Thus, in Gen. 17: Jahweh appeared (v. 1b)—Abraham fell on his face (v. 3)—and after the long speech of God, it only says "God went up from Abraham" (v. 22b). The speech of God in Gen. 35:9ff. is cast in the very same way: "God appeared to Jacob" (v. 9)—"Then God went up from him" (v. 13). Here, at long last, the disengagement from the cultic place is accomplished;

the appearance is now limited to the ceremonial framework of the speech of God. There is no longer any stress laid on the external detail involving the "appearances" of Jahweh. There is no direct line from the cultic-etiological speech to the conception of a theophany of Jahweh. The concept נראה is never utilized in the Old Testament for a cultic theophany.[13]

Rather, it reveals a completely different development of the concept: נראה is connected with a divine *speech of promise*. Already in the Jahwistic text, in Gen. 12 and 26, the specific content of the narrative is the promise of the possession of the land (12:7), or the blessing and the great numbers of descendants (26:24). Even in the present form of Exodus 3, which is conflated from Jahwistic and Elohistic elements, the primitive cultic etiology is linked with the narration of the call of Moses, which is oriented to the leading of the Israelites out of Egyptian slavery (vs. 7ff.). And the divine speech of promise in the priestly texts has reduced the old cultic-etiological elements to the periphery.

The speeches of Jahweh's self-manifestation are also encountered here, but they are entirely freed from the cultic-etiological pattern. This is made very plain in Gen. 18. The sentence: "And the Lord appeared to him by the oaks (or terebinths) of Mamre" (v. 1), is set as a heading or title for the story.[14] The presentation itself speaks differently about the manifestation of God and makes no use of the verb נראה. Thus, the introductory expression וירא יהוה clearly serves to qualify the *whole* narrative as a manifestation of God, though its decisive content is the promise of the son (vs. 10, 14). This tendency to make the introductory sentence independent occurs more and more frequently and is always linked with a promise,[15] which shows a movement away from the observable appearance, the manifestation of Jahweh, toward the proclamation of his activity.[16]

2. Clearly, the concept of a self-manifestation of Jahweh is in the end felt to be totally inappropriate.[17] In the priestly

document, when Abraham and Jacob are allowed to see a manifestation of אל שדי, the verb נראה is used in Gen. 17:1 and 35:11 with the formula אני אל שדי. However, in Ex. 6:3 it goes differently: "I appeared (נארא) to Abraham, to Isaac, and to Jacob, as God Almighty (El Shaddai), but by my name the Lord (Jahweh), I did not make myself known to them (לא נודעתי להם)." Here נראה is set over against נודע and there can be no doubt that this is done intentionally and is part of the very deliberate usage of the priestly document. The appearance of Jahweh is attributed to a preliminary stage, and with Moses something new is inaugurated: God allows himself to be known *as himself*. It is at this point in the priestly document that the name Jahweh is first used, and more is at stake than the simple communication of the name. Moses is obliged to begin his speech to the Israelites with אני יהוה (v. 6); the proclamation of the exodus out of Egyptian slavery, which follows in the next verse, ends with the formula, "and you shall know that I am the Lord your God" (v. 7); and at the end of the whole speech, which spans the time from the exodus to the entry into the promised land, there again stands the forceful: אני יהוה (v. 8). We have yet to undertake an investigation of the formula אני יהוה and what it means that Jahweh is to be known in his name.[18]

Our next task is to carry on the investigation of the concept נודע, for it is found in another linguistic context that is clearly distinct. This is in the Song of Zion in Psalm 48:3: "Within her citadels the Lord (Jahweh)[19] has shown himself a sure defense."

This expression is developed in the image of the invading king who will soon be fleeing in terror (vs. 5–7). נודע is used here in connection with a designation of Jahweh that characterizes him as the defender and helper of Israel in the face of its enemies. A related psalm, Psalm 76, begins with the sentence: "In Judah God (Jahweh) is known, his name is great in Israel" (v. 1).[20] It was developed in a sketch of the powerful and saving activity of Jahweh with Zion and its inhabitants. The same thing is said in the acrostic poem, Psalms 9/10: "The Lord (Jahweh) has made himself known, he has executed judgment; the wicked are snared in the work of their own hands" (9:16).[21] Jahweh proved himself as the judge of the godless, and, in the context of the psalm, he favors the pious, whom he defends and saves from their enemies. The proofs of Jahweh's power as defender and redeemer of Israel are here designated as his נודע, his making himself known. In the same sense, it can be said in third Isaiah that the *hand* of Jahweh is made known (Is. 66:14), and this means his saving activity in the return of the diaspora from exile and in the re-establishment of Jerusalem. There are many anthropomorphisms expressing Jahweh's power, such as: Jahweh allows his hand to be known (נודיע, Jer. 16:21); he allows his strong hand to be seen (הראה, Dt. 3:24), and the descending blow of his arm (Is. 30:30); his arm reveals itself (נגלה, Is. 53:1). The roots of words used in Old Testament speeches of revelation (all such to be found in later texts) are also used in this anthropomorphic sense. Still, the expressions "hand" and "arm" of Jahweh often exist in texts paired with concepts expressing Jahweh's power, such as: His power (Jer. 16:21), his greatness (Dt. 3:24), his wrath (Is. 30:30), 66:14). In this same line of thought are a whole group of texts in which these verbs are bound up with similar expressions: Jahweh's power, might and strength,[22] his help,[23] his דקה,[24] his חסד,[25], his כבוד,[26] and in summary, his נפלאות.[27] Psalm 98 is really a compendium of this way of speaking of Jahweh's power:

"O sing to the Lord a new song,
for he has done marvelous things (נפלאות)!
His right hand and his holy arm have gotten him the victory.
The Lord has made known (הודיע ישועתו) his victory,
he has revealed (גלה) his vindication (צדקה) in the sight of the nations.

∗He has remembered his steadfast love (חסד) and his faithfulness (אמונה) to the house of Israel.
All the ends of the earth have seen (ראה) the victory (ישה)
of our God" (vs. 1–3).

The point in all these texts is that Jahweh himself becomes
visible in his powerful acts of salvation. He becomes known
through these acts; whoever sees or experiences them can know
God in them. He becomes revealed in them.

There are many hymnic expressions that speak of Jahweh's
making himself known. In their general and universally valid
formulations, they could virtually be equal to expressions about
the essence of Jahweh: thus he is the one who makes himself
known in his acts of power (Psalm 98:2f.; 145:12). But this
is a late stage, in which various traditions have converged.
Often it is very expressly stated of definite and specific acts of
Jahweh that he is known in them; and especially about the
exodus out of Egypt, that fundamental act of salvation at the
beginning of the history of God with Israel: "Thou art the God
who workest wonders, who hast manifested (הודיע) thy might
among the peoples. Thou didst with thy might redeem thy people, the sons of Jacob and Joseph" (Psalm 77: 14f.; cf. 78:11ff.,
106:8ff.; Ex. 9:16; Dt. 3:24). It is disputed just how the accounts
of Jahweh's saving activity toward Jerusalem are to be understood in the Songs of Zion, Psalms 48 and 76 (cf. 46). It
is possible to see in them the ancient cultic-mythological
traditions of the assault of the nations on the city of God.[28]
Here, it is a totally different sphere of tradition involving the self-authentication of Jahweh in his own power. The
assurance that the cultic congregation in Jerusalem has is not
gained by directing its attention to a specific act in its past, but
to the tradition of the saving acts of Jahweh with the hope that
now and in the future he will save his city. In other passages,
the future is stressed. In the liturgical ending of the book of
Micah, there is the petition: "As in the days when you came

out of the land of Egypt I will show them marvelous things"
(Mic. 7:15; cf. Psalm 90:16). In other passages, the expectation
is for the powerful self-vindication of Jahweh in the return from
the exile and the reconstruction of Jerusalem (Is. 60:2, 66:14;
Psalm 102:17; cf. 85:8), and second Isaiah proclaimed the
imminent revelation of the כבוד of Jahweh which all flesh
will see (Is. 40:5).[29] The still imminent and future self-vindication of Jahweh comes more and more into the center of
expectation and hope. The earlier stress, especially the basic
one concerning the exodus from Egypt, is not forgotten, but it
can no longer be understood as the sole and ultimate self-
revelation of Jahweh. New and greater things are expected.
The full revelation of Jahweh has become an eschatological fact.

We have already pointed out that the niphal of ידע can be
found in two usages that are apparently distinct: in the disclosure of the name of Jahweh, and in the expressions about the
powerful self-disclosure of Jahweh through his historical acts
in the past, and in the future. In reality, they are not so distinct
from each other, and we can show this in the formula אני יהוה,
for it is completely rooted in the historical self-disclosure of
Jahweh.

3. Still, before this is done we have one more concept to
investigate, one which is found in passages just treated, namely,
כבוד יהוה. We can hardly avoid a discussion of it in our consideration of the Old Testament understanding of revelation,
because it expresses so clearly and so variously the manifestation of Jahweh himself.[30] We ought also to study passages
where an appearance or epiphany of the glory (כובד) is in the
world, and not just where it is a quantity connected or associated with Jahweh himself.

The oldest and most impressive expression is the cry of the
seraphim in the vision of Is. 6: "Holy, holy, holy, is the Lord
of hosts, the whole earth is full of his glory (כבוד)" (Is. 6:3).
This sentence is found in an interesting context in the history
of traditions. The heavenly beings surrounding Jahweh praise

his כבוד. This is reminiscent of similar expressions in various psalms: "The heavens are telling of the glory (כבוד) of God" (Psalm 19:1). In the parallel member of the verse: "and the firmament (רקיע) proclaims his handiwork." Here, as often, in the introduction to psalms, the heavenly sphere stands over and against the earthly.[31] It is in the heavenly world that one can speak of the כבוד of Jahweh, while in the earthly realm the stress is on the (visible) work of his hands. This is expressed in even sharper polarity in Psalm 29. Below, the activity of the thunderstorm is destruction and fear—whereas in the heavenly spheres of holiness everything cries: כבוד (v. 9b). Also, here the praise of the כבוד of Jahweh is limited to the heavenly regions.[32]

It is not just a coincidence that this usage (of כבוד) appears in the two psalms that are most Canaanite and thus most non-Israelitic in origin. In the heavenly pantheon, the כבוד of the God-King is praised, and on earth this is seen at best as a reflection in the works of creation.[33] There is a thoroughgoing reversal of usage in Is. 6 that in contrast has the כבוד of Jahweh filling the whole earth.[34] For the Israelite, the decisive aspect about the essence of God is his turning toward the world. Isaiah is not alone in this. Closely related is the expression of Psalm 97, which is stated in the framework of the same tradition: "the heavens proclaim his righteousness (צדק) and all the peoples behold his glory (כבוד)" (v. 6).[35] The fact that the כבוד fills the earth does not remain hidden, for it will become visible to all peoples.[36] In other passages the expression that Jahweh's כבוד fills the earth becomes formulated more often as a hope.[37] It was especially second Isaiah that proclaimed the powerful revelation of God which will be seen by "all flesh." (Is. 40:5).[38]

What does it mean when the כבוד of Jahweh becomes visible? In Is. 6, where the chant of the seraphim is recorded in its solemn and stark form, there is no explanation. However, in Psalm 97 the appearance of the כבוד is proof of the power of God, and the theophany is here set in a cultic framework.

This fits into the background of this tradition in which the thrust is on God's power being praised above that of all other gods and their worshipers. (vs. 7, 9). The peoples see it and are thereby incorporated into it. In second Isaiah and in the later texts, it is clearly evident that the manifestation of the כבוד of Jahweh means the public accomplishment of his power.[39] In second Isaiah, this proof of power is more decisively and fundamentally related to what constitutes God's being: "I am the Lord (Jahweh), that is my name; my glory (כבוד) I give to no other" (42:8; cf. 48:11). Here the idea of "honor" and "proof of power" are not to be separated from each other.

In contrast to this relatively fixed concept of the כבוד יהוה is the clearly distinct usage in the priestly texts of the Old Testament. In the priestly document of the Pentateuch, the כבוד is a spatial quantity, without precise limitations, which can from time to time descend from heaven, and in which Jahweh himself is present. It means that his appearance is "like a devouring fire" (Ex. 24:16f.); therefore he is constantly veiled in a cloud, and only Moses dared to enter into its midst. The place of the כבוד and its appearance in Ex. 24:15 is Sinai; from the erection of the אהל מועד, "the tent of meeting," onward, however, it is only at that place. Only in Ex. 16:7, 10, i.e. *before* the event at Sinai, do we hear that the כבוד appeared outside the encampment in the wilderness. Here, we ought to consider the connection from the point of tradition history. In Is. 6 and in Psalm 97, the כבוד concept was seen in connection with the temple tradition in Jerusalem. In both instances there were attendant phenomena, namely, the cloud (Psalm 97:2) and the smoke (Is. 6:4). Certainly, on the basis of this background, the כבוד concept of the priestly tradition must be seen as a specifically priestly extension of the tradition. This projection of the Jerusalem temple tradition back into the time of the wilderness is fully in accord with the conception of this document. In general, the individual elements in the transmission were used in a set framework. Most important, the כבוד is no longer something that proceeds from Jahweh, and in which he works; rather, it represents God in a much more massive sense, so that Jahweh himself is in it; thus, a speech of Jahweh always follows immediately upon an appearance of his glory (כבוד).[40]

The appearance of the כבוד is a rare experience of very special significance. In fact, these events can be divided into two distinct groups. In the first one, the כבוד appeared in order to present Jahweh's power over against the "murmuring" people and to support the one he had commissioned.[41] This usage is distinct from the nonpriestly tradition. Here, to "see Jahweh's כבוד" is not to see his proof of power in an unmediated way; which means that the כבוד appeared to give notice of the impending proof of the power of God. This clear recasting by the priestly tradition is especially meaningful. The כבוד has come to have such dignity that it remains in the background, in the cloud, as the initiator of the experience.[42]

In a second group of sayings, the appearance of the כבוד remains in a completely cultic context. Twice the fundamental instructions for the establishment of the cult were given on Sinai, and both times they were preceded by the appearance of the כבוד. In Ex. 24:15ff., the כבוד appeared on the mountain in order to give Moses instructions for the construction of the sanctuary (Ex. 25ff.). And after the construction was completed, the כבוד appeared in the sanctuary (Ex. 40:34f.) in order to transmit the laws of sacrifice to Moses (Lev. 1ff.).[43] And there is also a third time when the כבוד made its appearance, namely, when Aaron was about to complete the first offering. It was then the כבוד appeared as a fire coming from Jahweh and consuming the offering (Lev. 9:23f.).[44]

After this, the priestly document has no instance of an appearance of the כבוד in a cultic framework. Its task for the cult is fulfilled after it has established this and set it in motion.[45] Thus, even here the כבוד has a well-defined historical function. Ezekiel is clearly in the same tradition.[46] Also, here the כבוד is a spatially limited appearance that shines forth from the midst of a cloud (Ex. 1:4ff.). Also, for Ezekiel, the appearance of the כבוד is an event with a specific meaning. As Zimmerli has shown,[47] it is in this event that the prophet comes to the assurance that Jahweh is present among his people in exile even when they are absent from Jerusalem, and that he had abandoned idolatrous Jerusalem (11:22) and would return to the Temple again only in the final restoration of the city at the end of the age (43:1f.). Thus, Ezekiel's conception of the כבוד יהוה appears as a variation of the conception that is recognizable in the priestly document and is applied to the special situation at the end of time. The cultic continuity of Jahweh with the Temple in Jerusalem is broken, for Jahweh is present with his legitimate congregation in exile until the cult is truly restored in the Temple.[48]

Let us sum up. In the older conception, which was likely developed from the Temple tradition in Jerusalem, the כבוד of Jahweh, which was visible to all men, was praised. It is that aspect of the activity of Jahweh that could be perceived by men and in which he himself is revealed in his power. In the later development, especially since the time of deutero-Isaiah, the coming of this demonstration of Jahweh's power became the subject of the eschatological hope: its final and ultimate manifestation was awaited as the most imminent and decisive experience of the end time. In the priestly texts, כבוד is transformed into an unmediated representation of Jahweh. And even here it appears in order to announce Jahweh's demonstration of power (though only to Israel) and, moreover, in a special line of tradition also to establish and legitimate the cult. The seemingly reasonable and often expressed opinion that the כבוד in the priestly texts expresses a self-manifestation of Jahweh within the cult simply does not stand up on examination. On the contrary, from the priestly point of view, the appearance of Jahweh in his כבוד constitutes the establishment and the ordering of the cult, which alone makes possible the existence of the sinful people before God.[49]

II

The investigation of the texts which speak of the self-manifestation of Jahweh in connection with the root of ידע in the
niphal brings us to the formula אני יהוה as a specially pregnant
expression of the self-disclosure of Jahweh. If we pursue this
formula further, we could depend to a great extent on the
research of Zimmerli, who investigated the total complex of this
formula most thoroughly and who has substantially advanced
the understanding of its meaning.[50]

1. First of all, Zimmerli has presented the proof that the
formula אני יהוה is to be understood as an independent
sentence and therefore must be rendered: "I am Jahweh."
This is also valid for those expressions in which the formula is
linked with equivalents, as, for example, in the introduction to
the Decalogue, in which אנכי יהוה אלהיד ought to be rendered "I
am Jahweh, your God," and not "I, Jahweh, am your God."[51]

The sentence, "I am Jahweh" contains a self-disclosure
which Zimmerli designates as a "formula of self-representation."
In the ancient Orient such a self-representation is not unusual.
Gunkel has also correctly contended that the formula has its
origins in polytheism. The recipient of a manifestation of God
must ascertain *which* God is addressing him.[51a] Thus in the
oracles spoken to the Assyrian king Esarhaddon: "Fear not
Esarhaddon; I, the God Bel, speak to you," and "I am Ishtar
of Arbela, O Esarhaddon, King of Assyria."[52] One can also
expect such an understanding at an early stage of Israelite
religion. It is thus in two texts that belong in the class of
early presentations of the appearances of God.[53] In Exodus
3, Moses heard a voice out of the burning bush: "I am the
God of your fathers, the God of Abraham, Isaac, and Jacob,"
and the text continues: "then Moses hid his face" (v. 6). The
deity had presented himself, and he shrank back from this
confrontation. It is the same in Jos. 5, where Joshua saw a man
with a drawn sword and asked him if he were a friend or a foe.

The unknown person introduced himself as "commander of the army of the Lord." At this, Joshua fell down before him (vs. 13ff.). Only in these two passages does the self-presentation of God form an independent narration that has a special function in the context of the whole episode.[54] Thus one can speak of a self-presentation in a technical sense: the addressed person is made aware of the one in whose presence he is. Zimmerli's definition of the self-presentation formula is especially appropriate: "One who previously was unnamed emerges from his unknowability in allowing his name to be known and mentioned."[55]

This definition is not totally satisfactory for Ex. 3:6. The God who addressed Moses here designated himself as the God of his fathers. He is, therefore, not totally unknown at the time, but "presents himself as the familiar one by means of reference to things already known or to events in the past."[56] And these circumstances also obtain throughout the patriarchal material; with minor exceptions, the formula generally contains the expression "the God of your fathers."[57] In fact, the name of Jahweh can drop out completely, and not just in the Elohistic passages.[58] Even here the proof is rooted in the prior history of God with the fathers as the clearly decisive element; for the whole history of the guidance, blessing, and redeeming promise turns on the formulation "I am the God of your fathers." This is like the later formulation in Hosea, "I am the Lord your God from the land of Egypt" (12:10; 13:4), which echoes the whole of the Exodus tradition. The God who speaks here is the one who has already proved his power.[59]

However, the memory of the previous history is not an end in itself. In the patriarchal material, this formula is integrally related to speeches of promise.[60] The gaze is thus directed to coming events, though in connection with remembrance of previous activity of God. The event expected is in the future and is inserted into the whole previous history of God with the fathers. For the one passing on the tradition, it is not just the fathers who are involved, but the whole of Israel.

In light of all this, it is not accidental that the short formula אני יהוה appears without anything in opposition to it, only in the strictly cultic style of the later priestly texts in the Pentateuch and Ezekiel.[61] One ought to have reservations about seeing these as the original formulation, as Zimmerli does.[62] Rather, it appears as an abbreviation of the statement in an expression of most intense meaning. The name יהוה has all the overtones developed by such expressions in the older texts as: "I am Jahweh, the God of your fathers," "I am Jahweh, who has brought you out of Egypt," or in the theologically pregnant form, "I am Jahweh, your God."[63]

This reduction is especially evident in second Isaiah. Here one sees the אני יהוה in the most varied of contexts.[64] They all refer back to Jahweh's previous activity with or relationship to Israel. However, the simple אני אנכי יהוה is rarely seen. These are the passages in which the unique power of Jahweh is most sharply contrasted to that of other Gods, as "I am the Lord (Jahweh) and there is no other" (Is. 45:5, 6, 18). It is not that this God alone bears the name Jahweh in distinction from gods with other names. The name יהוה is rather a claim to power involving all that was developed in the polemic against the false gods.[65] It is much the same in other passages: "Was it not I, the Lord (Jahweh)? And there is no other god besides me" (45:21; see v. 5), or "I am the Lord, and besides me there is no savior" (43:11). And finally the name יהוה can drop out and be replaced by אל alone. "I am God, and there is no other" (45:22; cf. 46:9), or else אני יהוה ("I am it"—48:12; cf. 41:4, 43:10, 51:12). The short form presents the final pregnant coalescence of Jahweh's titles of power.[66] The development of this claim of power in second Isaiah occurs in the context of the evidence that God alone controls history—both the past that he had foretold and brought into being and the future that was just beginning. In summary, it would be: "I am the Lord (Jahweh), who do all these things" (45:7).

Nor is the short form the original one in the priestly texts. This

can be shown by the presence of the well-developed form in
Ex. 20 that introduces the Decalogue: "I am the Lord (Jahweh)
your God, who brought you out of the land of Egypt, out of the
house of bondage" (v. 2). And in the two Psalms that reflect
the event of the cultic proclamation of law there is likewise the
form of אלהד, or else the extended one referring to the Exodus
tradition (Psalm 50:7; 81:11). And God's law is therefore
proclaimed in express connection with the previous history of
Jahweh with Israel in which Jahweh is portrayed as the God
who continually leads and protects his people. The law obtains
its authority from this self-manifestation of God in the history of
Israel.[67] That is also clear in the legal formulations of the
priestly texts, especially in the series of commands in the ceremonial law where the formula אני יהוה appears at the *end*
of a single commandment.[68] The interpretation of the formula as
one of "self-introduction" is here eliminated. Rather, the name
יהוה must be here presupposed as known and carrying such
weight that commands emanating from this God have an
authority that is unambiguously binding.[69, 70]

2. The אני יהוה formula is moved into the sphere of revelation events, especially through the connection with the verb
ידע and the phrase ידע כי אני יהוה, "know that I am the
Lord." This "formula of acknowledgment" (*Erkenntnisformel*)
has been thoroughly investigated by Zimmerli,[71] and it is unnecessary to recapitulate this here. He has impressively shown
the variety of form and the consistency of meaning in this form
throughout the whole of the Old Testament, namely, that the
profession of God occurs only on the basis of his activity in
history. Begin with the sources of the Pentateuch, continue on
to the stories of the prophets in I Kg. 20, and end up with the
post-Ezekiel traditions! No matter, there is no variation in the
expression. Where there is an express profession of God, it
occurs in connection with his historical self-authentication.

Therefore, it is not strange that this formula is especially
prominent in the Exodus tradition. Here our observations on

the formula יהוה אני are confirmed. The strong professions (formula reduced to the short expression אני יהוה) can hardly be found in the older sources of the Pentateuch.[72] Instead, other forms appear to clarify the content of the acknowledgment: "That you may know, that there is no one like the Lord (Jahweh) our God" (Ex. 8:10); "that you may know that there is none like me in all the earth" (Ex. 9:14); "that you may know that the earth is the Lord's (Ex. 9:29); etc.[73] As stated above, the name itself is not the object of understanding, but the claim of power supported by it. The short formula must also be understood as a technical expression summing up this activity.

It is even clearer in the older texts how the knowledge of God is reached through God's action. As it is put at the end of the Jahwist's account of the destruction of the Egyptians in the Reed Sea: "And Israel saw the great work which the Lord (Jahweh) did against the Egyptians, and the people feared the Lord (Jahweh); and they believed in the Lord (Jahweh) and in his servant Moses" (Ex. 14:31). And in the contest of Elijah with the prophets of Baal on Mount Carmel, his offering was consumed by a fire coming down from heaven. "And when all the people saw it, they fell on their faces; and they saw it, they fell on their faces, and they said, 'The Lord (Jahweh), he is God the Lord (Jahweh), he is God' " (I Kg. 18:39).[74] Also Jethro the Midianite (Ex. 18:11: "The Lord (Jahweh) is greater than all gods.") and Naaman the Syrian (I Kg. 5:15: "there is no God in all the earth but in Israel.") acknowledged both the superiority and the uniqueness of Jahweh through what they had experienced and heard.

The sight and the experience of the acts of Jahweh brings about knowledge. These texts present it through a single event or limited chain of events. And in the introductory speech of the historical section of Deuteronomy, it is stated in retrospect on the whole previous history of Jahweh with Israel: "To you it was shown, that you might know that the Lord (Jahweh) is

God; there is no other besides him" (Dt. 4:35; cf. vs. 37–40).
The purpose of the whole history is to develop a knowledge of
God, a knowledge that only he is God and has power.

It is especially asserted of *future* events that they will produce
knowledge. The linking of ידע and אני יהוה are often found
with the final particle (chiefly למען), but especially in the per-
fect-with-waw consecutive that has a future sense: וידעת,
(וידעתם/וידעו) כי אני יהוה, "You will (he shall, they will) know
that I am the Lord (Jahweh)."[75] In the Exodus tradition, this
form of the designation is first encountered in the speeches of
Moses. This is in both the older and the newer strata of tradition. In the older Jahwistic epic, the stress is on the plagues
that were to bring Pharaoh and the Egyptians to a knowledge
of God (Ex. 7:17, 8:6, 18, etc.); in the newer priestly document,
the formulas of acknowledgment also appear in the report of the
destruction of the Egyptians in the Reed Sea (Ex. 14:4, 18).
Even here, the Egyptians themselves ought to acknowledge God
in this event; while Israel is to be led to an understanding of
God by means of the whole chain of events starting with the
exodus from Egyptian slavery to the occupancy of the land
promised to their fathers (6:7f.).[76]

For the rest it is almost exclusively in the prophetic sphere
that one finds the connection between the formula of acknowledgment and the events that are still imminent. The evidence
from the older prophetic tradition, such as that which is
transmitted in I Kg. 20, is very convincing. This passage
reports the rise of a prophet during the time of Ahab's war with
the Syrians. This prophet promised the king victory. "Thus says
the Lord (Jahweh), Have you seen all this great multitude?
Behold I will give it into your hand this day: and you shall know
that I am the Lord (Jahweh)" (v. 13). And again in the later
campaign of the Syrians: "Thus says the Lord (Jahweh),
'Because the Syrians have said "The Lord is a god of the hills
but he is not a god of the valleys," therefore I will give all this
great multitude into your hand, and you shall know that I am

the Lord (Jahweh)' " (v. 28). Jahweh's promise of victory,
which is natural in this tradition of the holy war, is here bound
up with the formula of acknowledgment.[77] God will be made
known through the victory accomplished in one specific battle.
Here it is especially clear that the formula אני יהוה is virtually
an abbreviation. Israel is to understand the victory as a new
self-manifestation of Jahweh. Here it is to be recognized that he
alone is God, and the victory is decided by Jahweh himself and
not by superior military might.

It is a noteworthy fact, too often overlooked in tradition
criticism, that this form of the prophetic speech concerning the
acknowledgment of God[78] first comes back into usage in the
two prophets of the exile who are in many respects quite different, namely Ezekiel and second Isaiah.[79] Still it has been profoundly transformed. In Ezekiel, the formula of acknowledgment is exclusively connected with words of judgment.[80] Israel
will experience God's self-vindication in the judgment that
it has brought on itself. One of the chief characteristics of
prophecy is the transformation of the old Israelitic traditions,
with their almost unbroken recitation of salvation, into expressions of judgment. This process is also reflected in the history
of the formula of acknowledgment. However, at the same time,
the perspective goes beyond the imminent judgment. It is not
God's last word; the history of Jahweh with Israel is not at an
end with judgment: "Then they shall know that I am the Lord
their God because I sent them into exile among the nations,
and then gathered them into their own land" (Ez. 39:28). The
last event which Ezekiel looks for is the restoration of Israel, and
in this event God is finally known: "Behold, I will open your
graves, and raise you from your graves, O my people; and I will
bring you home into the land of Israel. And you shall know
that I am the Lord, when I open your graves and raise you
from your graves" (Ez. 37:12f.).

Also, in second Isaiah, the statements of acknowledgment are
exclusively directed toward the self-vindication of Jahweh in

the future. God will be known through Cyrus, the executor of Jahweh's plan of judgment (45:3, 6) and through the final return of Israel (49:23, 26). In this way he will also demonstrate his own power over and against the other gods (43:10). The formula in second Isaiah does not have quite the same meaning as in Ezekiel, but it points in the same direction. This shows that historical self-vindication of Jahweh is more urgently awaited in the future to the extent that the hope of a new, final self-vindication of God comes to the fore.

3. It is not in the scope of this essay to pursue all the details of the Old Testament's expressions for acknowledging God,[81] but rather to concentrate on picking up a few of the most essential points for the understanding of the problem of revelation.

To understand the historical self-vindication of Jahweh, we must first give attention to one special observation: Throughout the entire history of the formula of acknowledgment, it is repeatedly asserted that the knowledge of Jahweh in his deity is intended not only for Israel, but for others as well. The plagues in Egypt ought to have caused Pharaoh (Ex. 7:17J) and the Egyptians (Ex. 117J, 7:5P) to acknowledge God. The priestly document also states that the Egyptians themselves ought to have acknowledged Jahweh through the destruction of their armies in the Red Sea (14:4, 18). Again and again, for Ezekiel, it is the people who ought to confess Jahweh in his demonstration of power, and as much in their own fate (25:7, 11, 17, etc.) as in the fate of Israel which they have witnessed (12:16, 36:23). The reference can be enlarged to include "all flesh" as those who ought to see and confess (21:4, 10). In second Isaiah, the perspective is distinctly broader. The activity of Jahweh is to bring about the acknowledgment of his deity not only for Cyrus (45:3), but for all peoples (43:10), for all "flesh" (49:26), indeed, from the rising to the setting of the sun (45:6).

The same content is dealt with in the above texts. Here, it is always Jahweh's demonstration of power that is observable and understandable to all the peoples and all the world. Let us take just two examples: Psalm 98:2f.: "The Lord has made known his victory, he has revealed his vindication (צדקה) in the sight of the nations. . . . All the ends of the earth have seen the victory of our God"; and Is. 40:5: "And the glory (כבוד) of the Lord shall be revealed, and all flesh shall see it together."

The revelation of Jahweh is not understood to be directed at only a special circle of men or to require a set of special presuppositions for its apprehension. All peoples, "all flesh," the ends of the world, see what happened, and its meaning as the self-vindication of God is accessible to them all. History is not here understood as the "aimed" activity of God, at least not in the sense that it is only "aimed" at Israel.[82] It is also not something penultimate which has only a subservient function in relation to the self-manifestation of Jahweh.[83] On the contrary, it has its fundamental meaning *as* a happening because in it God himself is manifested. This has only to be acknowledged by anyone who saw and experienced what happened. For this understanding of revelation everything depends on proceeding from the event, allowing it to have its full weight as an occurrence, and on focusing on the human response to the event as acknowledgment or rejection of God's self-manifestation.[84]

In this connection there is still one more question: How do *word* and event relate to each other in this understanding of revelation? It is clear that the formulas of acknowledgment are oral pronouncements authorized by Jahweh. In the Exodus tradition it is spoken by Moses, and elsewhere by the prophets. There is, of course, no question that the word has an essential connection with the event of revelation. However, in line with what has been previously said, the prophetic word itself is not to be taken as the revelation, for it is not Jahweh's own self-disclosure. The prophet's word points forward, or refers back to such a revelation by Jahweh. Acknowledgment is not brought about by the isolated word, but by the activity that the word proclaims and sees in its entire context in the historical tradition. There is no doubt that the acknowledgment of God

vindicating himself in historical activity goes back to the pre-
prophetic times of Israel's religion.[85] Before any confession is
brought about, it is of course true that history needs interpretation, or better, requires understanding. But this is not to be
a third party. The interpreter is not to be a mediator between
what happens and the one who experiences it. The activity
itself ought to bring about acknowledgment of God in the one
who observes the activity and understands it in its context as
an action of Jahweh. Especially in reference to the nations who
ought to acknowledge God in his activity, any attachment of
revelation to the prophetic word is from the outset excluded.
Of course, this implies nothing negative regarding the essence
of the prophetic word, nor is there any negative reflection on the
Old Testament concept of Word (דבר). In the perspective of
our thesis, both of these would still require a thorough and
sensitive study. These studies cannot be made in the framework
of the present essay, but I did feel obliged to make reference to
these limitations, in view of the understanding of revelation.

We have now examined many aspects of the Old Testament
understanding of revelation. The results as a whole, and also in
many specifics, go in a parallel course.[86] Throughout it is clear
that Jahweh is known in his historical acts to ancient Israel
and that in them he manifests himself as he is. In the second
part, it is especially clear that the Old Testament speeches
about the revelation of God are more and more anchored in the
future. From the time of the political catastrophe of 587 B.C.,
the conclusive self-manifestation of Jahweh was looked for as
the decisive event of the future. The old *heilgeschichtliche* traditions did not lose their value or importance. On the contrary,
they constituted the unconditional presuppositions for the
conclusive revelation of Jahweh in the future. Thus, the process
of revelation had begun in the earlier saving acts of Jahweh. In
these, Jahweh had always manifested himself as himself, and
Israel had lived on this self-revelation of his for centuries.
However, the experiences in its history also led Israel to the

understanding that the final revelation of God was yet to be
expected. The profound development in the faith and the
thought of Israel that has been accomplished by this alteration
would furnish material enough to write a theology of the Old
Testament, for the self-manifestation of Jahweh in history is the
font of all Israel's theology and faith. Thus, what is presented
here is but a section out of the total fabric of Israel's theological
thought and stands in close relationship to all the parts of this
totality.

Any theology of the Old Testament that would orient itself to
Old Testament thought patterns must proceed from an Israelite understanding of history and its historical development, but
it must also be fully acknowledged that at the time of the closing
of the Old Testament canon the history of Jahweh with Israel
and with the world is not to be understood as closed, but that it
is precisely these writings in the Old Testament that look on the
final revelation of Jahweh as still to come.[87]

NOTES

1. See p. 3.
2. W. Eichrodt, *Theologie des Alten Testaments*, 6th ed., 1959, 3 vols., Eng. trans.,
   Theology of the Old Testament (Westminster), 1961. Volume I is published.
3. O. Procksch, *Theologie des Alten Testaments*, 1950, p. 421.
4. L. Köhler, *Old Testament Theology* (Westminster), 1957.
5. E. Jacob, *Theology of the Old Testament* (Harper & Row), 1958.
6. Köhler, *op. cit.*, p. 54.
7. Also, Oepke began his article in Kittel's wordbook (*TWNT*, III, pp. 571ff.)
   with a section on "The Revelation of the Living God."
8. Th. C. Vriezen, *An Outline of Old Testament Theology* (Charles Branford).
9. Oepke (*TWNT*, III, pp. 573ff.) completely gave up on any explanation of
   the Old Testament usage and satisfied himself with a few remarks on the
   equivalents for ἀποκαλύπτειν in the LXX; H. Haag " 'Offenbaren' in der
   hebräischen Bibel" (*Th Z*, vol. 16, 1960, pp. 251–58), offers a very short
   lexicographical study that neither strives toward comprehensiveness, nor is
   carried on to any comprehensive clarification of the understanding of revelation.
10. ἀποκάλυψις does not appear in any theological sense in the LXX.
10a. Cf. *TWNT*, III, p. 573.

11. On the various usages of גלה, cf., for example, Gen. 35:7; I Sam. 3:7, 21; 9:15; Is. 40:5. Haag begins with the root גלה "because in it the primitive meaning of 'to reveal' is contained in its purest form. The fundamental meaning of גלה is undoubtedly 'to uncover,' 'to unveil,' that is to make free or visible something which is covered, veiled and therefore hidden" (*loc. cit.* p. 251). The theological "primal meaning" of "to reveal" is certainly not encountered in this way.

12. Cf. H. Gressman, *Moses und seine Zeit*, 1913, pp. 21ff.; M. Noth, *Exodus* (Westminster), 1962, see passage.

13. On the priestly concept of the appearance of כבוד יהוה see pp. 39f.

14. The original form of the account began like the one in Exodus 3, that is, with a statement of the circumstances: "As Abraham sat at the door of his tent in the heat of the day," and then continued with imperfect-with-waw consecutive. In contrast, וירא in Exodus 3:2 stands in the middle of a series of imperfects-with-waw.

15. Gen. 26:2f.; Jud. 6:12ff., 13:3ff.; I Kg. 3:5ff., 9:2ff.; cf. Ex. 3:16f.

16. This shift reflects a process that is most significant for the whole Israelite history of religion. The religious traditions native to the civilizations into which Israel generally entered were decisively transformed by the nomadic element that the Jews brought with them. The manifestation of the divinity at a particular place is a typical element of civilized religion, while the promise to a particular individual is an equally typical nomadic element. The latter has decisively stamped the tradition and differentiates Israel from its surrounding world. Cf. on this the classic statements of V. Maag, "Malkût jhwh" (*VT* Suppl. VII, 1960, pp. 129-53).

17. This can perhaps be seen in the use of נגלה. In the Elohistic tradition in Gen. 35:7, נגלה is used in reference to the appearance before Jacob in Bethel, where one might otherwise expect the use of נראה. A similar phenomenon can be seen in I Sam. 3:21, where נגלה stands along with נראה in a final sentence that clearly does not preserve the primitive Samuel tradition and that seems to be a correction in which נגלה is to replace נראה. נגלה itself is used in 3:7 in connection with the דבר יחוה.

18. The connection of נודע and אני יהוה can be found in the usage of Ezekiel (20: 5-9, 35:11ff., 38:23, 39:7) and in the later passage of Is. 19:21.

19. In the Elohistic rendition of the psalm read יהוה instead of אלהים.

20. See note above.

21. On this text cf. *BH*.

22. Ex. 9:6 (v. 15: Jahweh's hand); Psalm 77:15, (v. 16: Jahweh's arm), 106:8, 145:12.

23. ישועה: Psalm 91:16, 98:2f.; ישע: Psalm 50:23.

24. Is. 56:1; Psalm 98:2.

25. Psalm 85:8.

26. Is. 40:5, 60:2; Psalm 102:17.

27. Mic. 7:15; Psalm 78:11.

28. Cf. H. J. Kraus, *BK*, VX, Exkurs 5 on Psalm 46, pp. 342ff.

29. Third Isaiah's expectation is that Jahweh's צדקה *will* be revealed (Is. 56:1).

30. Cf. G. von Rad, *TWNT*, II, pp. 238ff.; and also B. Stein, *Der Begriff kebod jahwe und seine Bedeutung für die alttestamentliche Gotteserkenntnis*, 1939.

31. v. Rad, *op. cit.*, p. 243.

32. This understanding is also echoed in Psalm 113:4.

33. El is king in the Canaanite pantheon; cf. Psalm 29:10b. On Psalm 29:2, cf.
    the Ugaritic texts in which *kbd* (along with *šthwj*) belongs to the stereotyped
    form of the declaration of reverence before the throne of El (cf. Gordon,
    Ugaritic Manual, Text 49, I, 10; 51, IV, 26) and also other gods (51, VIII, 28f.
    2 Aqht V, 20, 30: 'nt III, 7; VI, 20). On the whole problem, see V. Schmidt,
    "Königtum Gottes in Ugarit und Israel," *BZAW* 80, 1961.

34. There are also heavenly beings who praise the כבוד. All this is clearly recog-
    nized in the tradition.

35. Cf. also Psalm 24:7-10: מלך הכבוד.

36. In a limited sense, the abbreviated expression "men who have seen my glory
    (כבוד)" (Num. 14:22) refers to the works of Jahweh where "signs" mean those
    that Jahweh did in Egypt and in the wilderness.

37. Num. 14:21; Psalm 72:19; cf. Psalm 57:6, 12 and 108:6, 102:16f.

38. Cf. the related expressions in third Isaiah (59:19, 60:1f., 66:18f.), the passage
    dependent on second Isaiah (35:2), and the verbal expression in 66:5.

39. In addition to the cited passages, see Psalms 138:5, 145:5, 11,12.

40. Ex. 16:10f.; Num. 14:10f., 16:19f., 17:7ff., 20:6f.; cf. also Ex. 24:16f., plus
    chap. 25ff. and 40:34f. plus Lev. 1ff., and see note 43 on this subject also.

41. Ex. 16:10; Num. 14:10, 16:19, 17:7, 20:6. This is also expressed in the citation
    in Lev. 10:3: "I will show myself holy among those who are near me, and
    before all the people I will be glorified (אכבד)"; on the character of this
    citation see Bertholet, on this passage.

42. In Ex. 14:4, 17, 18 (P) the destruction of the Egyptians is designated as
    Jahweh's "self-glorification" (כבד) over Pharaoh.

43. K. Koch has proved that Ex. 40:34f. does not simply relate the final appear-
    ance of Jahweh in his continual dwelling in the sanctuary, but rather intro-
    duces Lev. 1ff. See *Die Priesterschrift von Ex 25 bis Lv 16*, in *FRLANT*, 71, 1959,
    pp. 45f.

44. See Koch, *op. cit.*, p. 71, on the literary critical problem. In I Chr. 21:26 and
    II Chr. 7:1ff. this kind of occurrence is recorded in connection with David and
    Solomon. Koch, *op. cit.*, does not view these as a later gloss of the chronicler,
    but connects it with the older Jerusalem traditions. Also, compare I Kg 8:11,
    which belongs to the postdeuteronomic-levitical redaction (M. Noth, *Über-
    lieferungsgeschichtliche Studien*, 1943, p. 70, note 5; A. Jepsen, *Die Quellen des
    Königsbuches*, 1953, p. 102.)

45. The widespread opinion that the כבוד יהוה is the form in which Jahweh
    regularly appears in the holy place when it is used in the P document is rooted
    in an improper evaluation of the texts. On the one hand, אהל מועד in Ex.
    29:43 is spoken at the end of the instructions on the construction of the sanc-
    tuary: "There I will meet with the people of Israel, and it shall be sanctified
    by my glory (כבוד)." This expression exists all alone in an obviously secondary
    part of the account (see Noth on this passage) and is a usage not found in the
    rest of the priestly document. On the other hand, it says that Jahweh will meet
    Moses on the כפרת (the mercy seat which is over the ark). See Ex. 25:22, 30:6,
    and נועד in Ex. 29:43; and in Lev. 16:2 there is the generalized expression:
    "in the cloud upon the mercy seat כפרת." כבוד is nowhere linked with כפרת.
    Both clearly belong to distinct complexes of traditions that have not been
    linked together. Only in Lev. 16:2 is there a later formulation that implies
    such a combination when it speaks of the "cloud." But here too it is only after

the giving of the law to Moses (cf. Ex. 25:22) that the appearance of Jahweh on the mercy seat (כפרת) is expected.

46. Only in Ex. 39:21, and then in the verbal form in 28:22 and 39:13, is כבוד used in the sense of a public demonstration of the power of Jahweh.

47. *BK*, XIII, pp. 58, 84.

48. P speaks only of the time in the wilderness, but II Chron. 7:1ff. acknowledges that in the Jerusalem tradition the establishment of the cult was legitimized by means of the כבוד יהוה. See note 44.

49. See K. Koch, "Die Eigenart der priesterschriftlichen Sinaigesetzgebung" in *ZThK*, vol. 55, 1958, pp. 36–51, esp. 41ff.

50. W. Zimmerli, "Ich bin Jahwe," in *Geschichte und Altes Testament, Festschrift Alt*, 1953, pp. 179–209; *Erkenntnis Gottes nach dem Buche Ezechiel*, 1954; "Das Wort des göttlichen Selbsterweises (Erweiswort), eine prophetische Gattung," in *Mélanges Bibliques, rédigés en l'honneur de André Robert*, 1955, pp. 154–64.

51. *Festschrift Alt*, pp. 181f.

51a. *HK* on Gen. 17:1.

52. J. B. Pritchard, *Ancient Near Eastern Texts*, Princeton, N.J., 1955, p. 450; also *ACT*, 2nd ed.; pp. 281ff.; *ANET*, p. 450.

53. See p. 33.

54. Both texts are originally sanctuary etiologies; cf. the almost equivalent sentence in Ex. 3:5b (in the parallel J text) and Jos. 5:15a.

55. *Festschrift Alt*, pp. 179f.

56. Zimmerli, *loc. cit.*, p. 194. Both formulations exist alongside each other without any balancing. The Babylonian oracle also has a reference to one already known.

57. This expression is missing only in Gen. 31:13 ("I am the God of Bethel") and in 15:7, where the אני יהוה is developed by the clause "Who brought you from Ur of the Chaldeans." Gen. 15 could also be an evidence of deuteronomic redaction; cf. O. Kaiser, *ZAW*, vol. 70, 1958, pp. 107ff.

58. An example of this is Gen. 26:24, where יהוה is used in the beginning of the verse.

59. See K. Elliger, "Ich bin der Herr—euer Gott," in *Theologie als Glaubenswagnts, Festschrift für Karl Heim*, 1954, pp. 9–34.

60. An explicit promise is missing in Gen. 31:13; still, the command to depart is at once the expression of divine guidance. In Ex. 3, both of the sources continue with a promise (J v. 7; E v. 9).

61. On Gen. 15:7 see note 57.

62. *Festschrift Alt*, p. 182. After the investigations of Elliger, one can hardly maintain the hypothesis that the formula אנכי יהוה אלהיכם in the prologue to the Decalogue represents the merging of two primitive independent elements (*Mélanges Bibliques*, p. 159, ftn. 3).

63. Cf. K. Elliger, *op. cit.*, p. 32.

64. Cf. Zimmerli, *Festschrift Alt*, pp. 198f.

65. Cf. Is. 42:8 "I am the Lord (Jahweh), that is my name, my glory (כבוד) I give to no other."

66. The ring of this short form is to be distinguished from the definitions employed by Ellinger in his distinctions between formula of "holiness," or "majesty," and "*Heilsgeschichte*," or "homage." *op. cit.*, p. 15, etc.

67. Cf. Elliger, *op. cit.*, p. 32. The cultic theophany is also first legitimated through the historical reference (Ex. 19f.; Psalms 50 and 81).

68. Esp. in Lev. 18 and 19. On the reconstruction of the series of commandments, cf. G. v. Rad, *Studies in Deuteronomy* (SCM Studies in Biblical Theology, no. 9), pp. 25ff.; and K. Elliger, *ZAW*, 67, 1955, pp. 1–25).

69. K. Elliger has shown that the historically oriented framework of Lev. 18 calls for the form compounded with אלהיכם, while the Law itself calls for the short form (*Festschrift Heim*, pp. 11ff., and *ZAW*, 67, 1955, esp. pp. 23ff.).

70. The question of the original *Sitz im Leben* of the אני יהוה formula cannot be thoroughly discussed at this point. On the basis of the late priestly tezts, Zimmerli is of the opinion that the theophany speeches ought to be the original *Sitz im Leben*, especially those of the cultic proclamation of the Law. Elliger has already raised some objections to this (*ZAW*, 67, 1955, p. 25). In any case, it must be emphatically stated that the formula is closely connected with the *heilsgeschichtliche* traditions. The idea of a theophany as the original *Sitz im Leben* needs additional investigation, especially in view of the older texts in the Pentateuch. More investigation is also needed on whether the prophetic "words of authentication" stem from "the central liturgical event of the self-presentation of Jahweh" (Zimmerli, *Mélanges Biblique*, p. 160). This is especially true from the point of tradition criticism.

71. *Erkenntnis Gottes, passim.*

72. In the pure form only in Ex. 7:17, 10:2(J); cf. 8:18.

73. Cf. Zimmerli, *Mélanges Biblique*, pp. 23ff.

74. In verse 37 Elijah prays: ". . . that this people may *know* that you, O Lord (Jahweh), art God."

75. Cf. Zimmerli, *Erkenntnis Gottes*, for the individual examples.

76. The distinction that has been worked out by Elliger to distinguish "formulas of majesty" and "formulas of homage" is also recognizable in the priestly writing (Pg), though Elliger himself denies it (*Festschrift Heim*, pp. 29f.). Note that in connection with the expressions of knowledge involving the Egyptians, there is the simple אני יהוה (Ex. 7:5; 14:4, 18), while for Israel it is אני יהוה אלהיכם (6:7, 16:12; cf. 29:46a).

77. Psalm 46:11 also shows the connection between the formula of acknowledgment and the tradition of the holy war.

78. Zimmerli has designated the form of prophetic speech that ends with a concluding formula of acknowledgment by the term "word of proof" (*Erweiswort*). This is especially evident in I Kg. 20 and Ezekiel (*Mélanges Bibliques*, pp. 154ff.). From a form-critical point of view, second Isaiah is not in this tradition (cf. Zimmerli, *Erkenntnis Gottes*, pp. 31f.).

79. The formula of acknowledgment is not essentially different from Hosea's and Jeremiah's use of the root ידע. Cf. H. W. Wolff, *Ev. Theol.*, 12, 1952/3, pp. 533–54; 15, 1955, pp. 426–31.

80. Zimmerli, *Erkenntnis Gottes*, pp. 69ff.

81. Among other things, we are now close to the concept of אות, "sign." C. A. Keller (*Das Wort OTH als "Offenbarungszeichen Gottes*," Dissertation, Basel, 1946) has undoubtedly overemphasized the meaning of the concept, but there is a relation between אות and revelation. Here, the discussion will be limited to two points: on the one hand, the emergence of the concept in the Exodus tradition, occasionally in connection with the expressions of acknowledgment (for example, Ex. 8:18f., 10:2; cf. Keller, pp. 29ff., 117ff.), and on the other hand, with the development of אות in the postexilic time into an eschatological

concept (e.g. Is. 55:13, 66:19; Keller, pp. 115ff.). Thus, the main lines of the history of this concept parallel those of the understanding of revelation.

82. Zimmerli, *Erkenntnis Gottes*, pp. 66f.: "The happenings which the prophet reported . . . were happenings aimed at the people of God." H. W. Wolff, "Die Geschichtsverständnis der alttestamentlichen Prophetie," (*Ev. Theol.*, 20, 1960, pp. 218–35): "History for prophecy is the discussion of the Lord aimed at the future of Israel" (p. 222).

83. Zimmerli, *Erweiswort*, p. 158.

84. There are expressions in the prophetic books that are undoubtedly aimed at producing repentance as the result of a happening. For example, Amos 4:6ff. (cf. Wolff, *op. cit.*, pp. 219ff., on this point). However, where there is the explicit reference to the self-manifestation of Jahweh, the above assertion must be maintained.

85. Cf. Wolff, *op. cit.*, p. 229, note 17.

86. There is not time here to point out the variety of cross-references between the individual parts of the paper, but many are self-evident in the text itself.

87. A radically shortened form of this essay appeared in *ThLZ*, 85, 1960, pp. 833–38.

III

The Understanding of Revelation Within the History of Primitive Christianity

Ulrich Wilkens

Our investigation of the understanding of revelation in primitive Christianity ought to begin by studying the terms for revelation in the New Testament, but this will be bypassed. First of all, there is no correspondence between the many New Testament terms that can be translated "revelation," "to reveal," or "revealed," and the use of these terms in modern protestant theology. In addition, the modern concept of revelation does not do justice to the Greek terminology, and it also exceeds the *terminological* sphere of the New Testament's conception of revelation, that is, terms which do not need to be translated "revelation" still belong to the *subject matter* of this concept. So the entire terminological range of ἀποκάλυψις, ἀποκαλύπτειν, φανεροῦν, etc., will be included in this investigation, but it will also go beyond the scope of these concepts. The longer one proceeds with an investigation of the terminology, the clearer it is that the question as to what "revelation" means must be decided beforehand and serve as a criterion for the choice of the New Testament passages to be taken into account. We will take as our starting point a survey that deals with the terminology: the excellent article by Hannelies Schulte.[1] The question to begin with is not: What is the meaning of the New Testament terms that are translated into English as "revelation," and what kind of common meaning will emerge from them? Such procedures would lead to either recognizing various concepts of revelation or developing an ambiguous generalized one. This general concept is found in contemporary investigations of the history of religion and produces little clarity in the understanding or discrimination of the facts. For clarity, the question must be critically put: Is there anything in the primitive Christian tradition that in substance would correspond to the term "revelation" in its current technical theological usage?

The theological concept of revelation in a strict sense is presented in the first essay by Wolfhart Pannenberg,[2] and is presupposed in this essay. Accordingly, the term "revelation" in what follows designates the *complete self-disclosure of God*. Consequently, the self-revelation is necessarily one and to be distinguished from mere appearances of God. The form of its occurrence is consistent and does not vary. Revelation is at the same time essentially universal insofar as it is the *self*-revelation of *God*. The present concern then is: Does the New Testament have anything that in substance approximates such a concept of revelation? And if this is the case, to what event is this type of revelation related in the primitive Christian tradition? And finally, how is this revelatory event and the relation of the Christian to it understood in the various spheres of tradition and their theological positions?

So put, the problem of understanding revelation in primitive Christianity encompasses from the outset the entire history of primitive Christianity as this has grown out of the Jewish sphere of tradition and penetrated the diversity of the Hellenistic world. Accordingly, the procedure is as follows: (1) The investigation will originate with the understanding of revelation in Judaism. (2) With an understanding of the historical origins of Judaism, our search will then turn to Jesus and the original Palestinian congregations and show here how the resurrection of Jesus in connection with his previous claims to authority became known as the unique and final self-revelation of God; from this point on the attention will be directed to the understanding of this revelatory event. (3) We ask the question what revelation means in the context of Hellenistic Christianity and especially Paul; (4) then in the context of the theological conceptions of Mark and Luke; (5) the writer of Hebrews; and finally (6) the fourth evangelist.[3]

1. THE UNDERSTANDING OF REVELATION IN JUDAISM

The Old Testament essay of Rolf Rendtorff has shown that the self-revelation of Jahweh originally was recognized in the past acts of Jahweh, then in the prophets became more and more something to be expected in the future, an impending act of Jahweh.[4] When second Isaiah waits for the final and decisive coming of Jahweh from the wilderness (see the introduction to the book, Is. 40:5), he uses the term כָּבוֹד, "Jahweh as that which all flesh will see." We are here dealing with usage in the tradition of Israel's concepts that is the closest thing to an unmediated revelation of God himself.[5] Jahweh is surrounded by his glory, which is all the brightness associated in Ezekiel with the emerging figure of Jahweh in the vision of the throne chariot (Ez. 1:28): "Such was the appearance of the likeness of the glory of the Lord." Among other things, one can see this vision as a very bold conception: Jahweh has abandoned Jerusalem, but just as the new day of the future dawns, it will come to be that "the glory of the God of Israel came from the east . . . and the earth shone with his glory," and Jahweh will enter Jerusalem and the new temple (Is. 43:1ff.).[6]

The movement, which here takes place in an analogous way in Ezekiel and second Isaiah, clearly demonstrates the general direction that caught hold of subsequent developments in Judaism's history of theology. That is, *the whole of Judaism expected the decisive, saving, self-revelation of Jahweh in the eschatological future.* This does not in any way contradict the fact that from the time of the restoration of the temple to its destruction in A.D. 70, the cult in Israel carried on its ancient practice and continually celebrated the acts of God in the time of the patriarchs that established Israel as the congregation of God. While in this respect the temple remained the center of the traditional community, and even if the early great acts of Jahweh were given constitutive meaning in view of the election of the present celebrating community, at the same time the

self-revelation of Jahweh was no longer recognized in those
events, or even in anything known in the past, but was much
rather expected as something in the eschatological future.
The prayers of the synagogue worship and the daily prayers of
the pious were directed to Jahweh as one who was in the eschatological future. Of course, Jahweh was addressed as "the God
of Abraham, Isaac, and Jacob,"[7] but precisely as such he is pre-
eminently מְחַיֵּה הַמֵּתִים, "Jahweh, who brings the dead to life."[8]
The daily prayer is for a permanent renewal of the holy and
primordial time in the eschatological gathering of Israel and
the destruction of all its enemies. This is the time of (הֵרוּת and
גְּאֻלָּה), of the freedom and redemption of Israel.[9] Along with
this in the same prayer is a petition for the continued dwelling
of Jahweh in Zion as the "house of your glory,"[10] but this is not
connected with the eschatological restoration and is clearly a
concern of second rank in the prayer as a whole.

It is obvious in this Jewish liturgical material that the fundamental direction of all pious lives is directed toward the eschatological future. This is also universally true for all early Judaism.
Since that time, Judaism has not lost this fundamental eschatological motif. It can be found in apocalyptic as well as Rabbinic
material. Prayers like the one cited above have been prayed by
theologians and laity in both ancient and later Judaism.

Yet, essential differences are perceptible with reference to the
understanding of the self-revelation of Jahweh in its relation
to the meaning and the function of the *Law*. While it may not
be representative of the total tradition of early Judaism, one
can find in most of Rabbinic scholasticism the exegetical
judgment that Israel "possesses in the Torah a normative
revelation which is valid for all time."[11] Under such a judgment, complete knowledge of the Law achieves a clarity of
revelation that cannot be surpassed by the final events. In
fact, the giving of the Law to Moses is considered in Rabbinic
theology to be *the* revelation of the will of Jahweh which has
happened once and for all (ἐφ' ἅπαξ). In the Law, every possible

situation has been taken into account to the extent that the eye of the Torah is the all-seeing omniscience of God, and all righteous life is oriented toward the divine commandments laid down in the Torah, a Law valid for all time. According to Rabbinic understanding, the moment on Sinai is understood in the strictest sense as the "midpoint of time" (*Mitte der Zeiten*), which is confirmed but not surpassed at the "end of time." The past event on Sinai had this character on account of the *eternal* Torah, which is the will of God since the time when it was given to Moses, and which is, as the will of God, present and understandable in time. The *eschaton* cannot give more than the Law is able to give. Thus, when the pious Jew in obedience to the Law "does take the yoke of God's kingly rule upon himself," and prays for the "revelation" of the kingly rule of God at the end of time, a change in the present situation of the faithful is meant:[12] the falling away of all enemy rule and the complete realization of life according to the Law. All of this does not in substance exceed the gift already given on Sinai. Two things are to be considered here. One, the Rabbinic eschatology remained predominantly within a nationalistic framework. Two, the end of the Temple worship in A.D. 70 was viewed as an outer, not an inner tragedy. The cult was dispensable in a situation where the Law had for a long time been the only universal and definitive manifestation of Jahweh. All of the revelation of God, past, present, and future, was concentrated in the Law.

Actually, the Law, as understood Rabbinically, is not a *self*-revelation of God in the strict sense of the word. The Rabbinic theologians did indeed see the divine glory over the Torah, and they spoke of its preexistence and eternity; but the Law did not have the function of revealing God himself to man, but rather the fulness of his will for the man who would be righteous before Jahweh. The context of Rabbinic theology simply had no place for the self-revelation of Jahweh, either on Sinai or in the *eschaton*. On the contrary, there was an increasing

tendency in Rabbinic theology to stress the absolute inap-
proachableness of God to the extent that the structure of Rabbinic theology excluded any revelation of Jahweh. This
corresponds to the striking fact that in the sphere of Rabbinic
theology the whole *heilsgeschichtliche* tradition of ancient Israel,
with its meaning as a creed based on the history of election,
was profoundly altered. It has been changed into a picture book
of holy and legitimated examples of how the Law is fulfilled
(or not fulfilled).[13] Outside of creation, Rabbinic thought knew
of only one activity of God: the giving of the Law on Sinai.

Dietrich Rössler has shown how different the popular theology
of the early Jewish era is from that presented in the apocalyptic literature and the Qumran documents. Jewish apocalyptic has preserved the heritage of the prophets, although in a
variety of ways. That which has been preserved is the fundamental orientation to the eschatological future, which is
conceived as the impending, unique, and all-inclusive self-
revelation of Jahweh, and which has found a theologically
consistent form of expression in a new conceptual framework.
But also here the Israelite tradition of *heilsgeschichtliche* motifs
has been weakened. Its only place was probably in the cult
shown in some of the later historical Psalms. However, the
constitutive element of all *heilsgeschichtliche* structures is
retained in the apocalyptic theology, namely, the basic conception of election as the fundamental historical act of God,
through which all of the Israelitic history takes on the character
of election history. The election of God constituted the small
band of righteous as the saved congregation in the midst of
enmity of the blasphemers. The fate of this group demonstrated
the truth of the election and the faithfulness of God by directing
all theological attention to the end of this age when the elect
congregation will have been rescued from the oppression by
enemies and brought at last into the peace of the final salvation.
The goal of the elect community's history is also the goal of this
age (in modern terms, the end of all history), in the degree that

God directs all destiny to the goal of historically confirming the
election according to his saving purpose which he began to
work out in the original election. This is expressed as follows:
From the beginning of time, God has held in secret all the
eschatological gifts of salvation for the chosen righteous ones.
They are held in readiness for "revelation" on the last day to
prove the truth of election and of God himself.[14] The interim
giving of the Law is a sign of the community's election insofar as
the Law in its commandments has only one single purpose:
to help the people remain faithful to the God who chose them
during the time of this age and throughout all affliction. Thus,
in apocalyptic understanding, the Torah itself has no revelatory
character, although along with its demands for men it also
witnesses to the validity of the gift of being chosen and to the
process and goal of history as having its meaning in continuing
election. He has grasped the real meaning of the Law who here
and now keeps it in its radical form and who in such faithfulness expresses his trust in the election which determines history
and the final victory. The apocalyptic theology is completely
oriented to this end as the final and valid judgment of God,
which includes both election and its history. Everything depends on the hope that the gifts of salvation now hidden in
heaven will be truly revealed. Thus, it is not just the salvation
of the righteous (whose salvation is the historical ratification of
election) that is at stake, but the very belief in God himself.
In this aeon, the compelling power of the evil ones works as a
negative experience on the just, whose salvation is hidden for
the time being. Thus, because the righteous, who have been
elected, will one day receive the gifts of salvation, it is God
himself who will demonstrate in his righteous judgment who
he is, namely, the one who has elected his people. With this in
mind, apocalyptic theology is exclusively directed toward a self-
revelation of God in its strictest sense. But one example of this
would be the eschatological hymn in Eth. Enoch 63:2f., in
which the hymn in praise of God is to be understood in the

sense of the final eschatological participation in the gifts of salvation: "May he be praised, the Lord of the spirits . . . , the Lord of *glory* and the Lord of wisdom, before whom every secret is known [that is, every gift of salvation which has been kept in secret]." The revelation of the gifts of salvation in connection with their appropriation by the righteous is synonymous with the revelation of the glory of God. This could be verified by supplementary evidence from the Qumran literature. 1QM 1:16 says: "The glory of God together with the host of the holy ones [angels] appears as help . . . truth for the destruction of the sons of darkness." The text is not clear at this point, but the conception can be verified through parallel passages: In the final act of the eschatological battle, the unshielded glory of God will be engaged and two things will happen. First there will be aid and salvation for the children of light, and at the same time there will be destruction for the sons of darkness.[15] Thus, in the last analysis, the common viewpoint of apocalyptic theology equated the eschatological reception of the gifts of salvation with the reception of the glory of God himself (also glorification δοξασθῆναι),[16] because all the gifts of salvation have the character of participation in God, that is, of having the Kingdom of God with its life, joy, peace, etc. The entrance of the just into the eschatological salvation and life is entrance into the splendor that surrounds God himself. This is not to say that such participation would damage or dissolve the distinction between God and man, for that would be to take apocalyptic eschatology into the schema of Hellenistic mystery religions, as Philo or the Christian gnostics in Corinth did.[17] The apocalyptic did not know of such an identification with God because participation in salvation is understood as an act of God analogous to God's initial election. What is presupposed in the final participation of the just in the salvation of God is that God's glory is revealed to the elect through an act of God. To have part in the glory of God in the eschatological sense is to have a direct part in the final election (which, in apocalyptic language, is no longer "hidden," but "revealed"). The recipients of salvation are eternally and unequivocally elected by God.

It would be from this center that the various attempts of apocalyptic theology could be understood in their effort to gain perspective on the course of history in view of its goal. Such attempts, and all the mythical imagery that goes with such epic-like sketches of history, are attempting to mark out the place of the present between the past and the future. It is an admission of a fundamental misunderstanding to reject such apocalypses as Oepke does by judging them to be "confused imagery," "having little in common with true prophesy which reveals the will of God in history and clarifies his moral will."[18] Such a judgment flatly rejects what the apocalyptic theologian is trying to do. The "confused imagery," or mythical presentations,[19] show that the apocalyptic wishes to describe the history of election from the perspective of its end point, or goal. This is distinct from the prophets who reject such a scheme of history in favor of a cultic *heilsgeschichtliche* framework founded on the past history of Israel. But the two are not so distinct. Think of the spontaneous proclamation of the prophets regarding the specific acts of God, all of which are possible only on the basis of specific visions and messages given by God at the time. Think of recipients of the apocalyptic revelation and what they see and hear, and how it corresponds in content and manner of knowing to the visions and words that make up the eschatological revelation. The apocalyptic visions and messages have the character of an anticipated eschatological unveiling.[20] Today this is widely overlooked where the intention of the apocalyptic texts falls under the theological verdict. Their intention was to make the divine plan of the whole of history into the criterion for the presentation of history, with the stress not on calculating the divine plan, but on submitting it for the freedom of the divine activity, which in principle cannot really be predicted.[21] Such general evaluation, apart from the systematic problems it would

involve, can only be made historically if one categorizes all the
claims to proleptic-eschatological revelation as just so much
"calculation" about, or "decorative trappings" of the end
event. The God of apocalyptic theology is a free being who can
act in the light of changing circumstances. On the one hand, he
has revealed his final activity before the time to the apocalyptic
visionary, but on the other hand, it is he alone who engages in
such activity, and his ability to act is in no way inhibited by the
proleptic revelation itself.

However, with such a judgment, the inner connection is
broken in the linkage between the Jewish apocalyptic and Jesus
of Nazareth in his historical situation. His proclamation may
have been quite restrained in the use of certain traditional
concepts, compared with all the apocalyptic witnesses we have.
Still, if the personal demand of Jesus, which made its impact
through his words and deeds, is to be understood, then we must
at least refer to the claim of proleptic-eschatological "revelation" in apocalyptic theology as his own overarching historical
presupposition.

2. Revelation in the Appearance and Fate of Jesus

Jesus of Nazareth was no Rabbi.[22] His preaching and teaching could not be explained from the background of Rabbinic
theology. Jesus surely knew Rabbinic theology, but his manner
of thinking does not bear this stamp. His teaching and proclamation should rather be characterized by a deliberately anti-
Pharisaic and anti-Rabbinic polemic. The expression "Scribes
and Pharisees" seems to be the general characterization for the
opponents of Jesus. This seems to be a historically accurate
conclusion in view of the great number of clashes they had with
him. Jesus is also constantly attacking them in the tradition we
have, and this appears to represent a fundamental tendency.
There isn't any point in classifying this as intramural debate
either—as though Jesus was out to attack a particular thesis

of the Rabbis, or a given practice of the Pharisees. Jesus was out to confront their presuppositions, their fundamental intent and point of departure. There is one particular text which would make this clear. It is sharply put, is helpful for our total discussion, and is representative of the entire anti-Pharisaic tradition. The text is Mt. 5:21–22a: "You have heard that it was said to men of old, 'You shall not kill; and whoever kills shall be liable to judgment.' But I say to you that every one who is angry with his brother shall be liable to judgment." Verse 21 is stated according to Rabbinic form.[23] The prohibition of the Torah that was delivered on Sinai and handed on to all following generations is also the constitutive element of the binding teaching of the "men of old." As verse 21b demonstrates, the method of Torah interpretation is to develop the meaning and the sphere of applicability without altering the words. This is founded on the understanding that all truth is once and for all spoken in the Law. The "scribes" have their task limited to the delineation of the present situation which is still controlled by the letter of the law. In the perspective of the Decalogue, the threat of punishment for the murderer is exclusively eschatological in character.[24]

In these antitheses, Jesus is using the outer form, but not the inner reasoning of Rabbinic debate. The manner of the argumentation is to a very large degree shaped by the Rabbinic style, in which the introductory formula, "but I say to you," can often be found in Rabbinic disputes.[25] At the same time, these are still the arguments and teachings of a man who is standing in the face of the whole way of teaching employed among "the wise men."[26] Such an opposition is possible, but is developed under two presuppositions: (1) The contradictory assertions used against the majority opinion must be as much in formal agreement with the letter of the Torah as is the opinion of the majority; (2) The validity of the teaching of "the wise men" must not be questioned. When a Rabbi uses the expression, "but I say to you," it would be impossible for him to reject the teaching of "the men of old." Mutually exclusive assertions are impossible in Rabbinic theology because any true assertion is grounded in a word of scripture. Jesus, however, is thinking in terms of mutual exclusion. The ἐγὼ δὲ λέγω ὑμῖν sets up a contradiction to the established teaching without citing a new passage from scripture so that the new statement would emerge out of the other statement in the Decalogue in a harmonious fashion. The old prohibition and the old definition of punishment would then be harmonized with the new statement against anger and its penalty. Seen in the framework of the formal structures of argumentation, we can note that Jesus is not attempting to establish an antithesis that will supplement the teaching of "the men of old." Jesus is rejecting the old tradition. He could have found a statement in the Torah to undergird his discussion on anger, but he chooses instead to base his position on his own claim to authority. He is using the debate style of Rabbinic tradition precisely for the purpose of polemics. In the very place where a Rabbi would use the Torah in developing the Halacha, we find Jesus using the simple ἐγώ. Let us grant that this is not against the content of the Law of Moses as such, but against the tradition of Rabbinic interpretation. Nevertheless, even this distinction between the Law and the tradition about the Law, or between the content of an argument and its formal aspects, is a distinction that is impossible in Rabbinic theology and strikes at its very foundation. The Rabbi would see this argument as a rejection of what the Law forbids in favor of a new prohibition, which is tantamount to rejecting the authority of the Torah in favor of a new authority. This statement was meant to be understood in this Rabbinic way to accentuate the polemics! Rabbinic theologians would gladly enter into a discussion on whether a man who hated his brother was guilty of the eschatological damnation due a murderer—just as long as new citations from scripture were brought into the discussion. However, it would be unthinkable for these same theologians to enter into any such discussion when the authority for a new interpretation was nothing but the personal authority of Jesus. In their understanding, the formal manner of argumentation is itself cause for charging Jesus with blasphemy. "It was said . . . you shall not kill" is a statement coming from the mouth of God himself.[27] In contrast, the one who issues the command against anger is Jesus himself. His use of the ἐγώ means he puts himself in the place of God. Thus, the claim which Jesus makes in his antithesis against the Rabbinic tradition could not possibly presuppose this type of tradition as its historical origin. Jesus is not arguing here as a Rabbi would. The question is to explain this claim of Jesus from a historical point of view. It is necessary to state this question even when a concrete answer seems next to impossible because of the lack of any contemporary analogies in the world of that day. However, this is no cause for allowing the historical question to die on the vine. What of the assertion of the uniqueness of Jesus' self-consciousness at this point?

There is no proof in the Jewish theological history of any phenomena that could be comparable to the anti-Pharisaic polemic of Jesus.[28] There is no option but to allow that Jesus had a very unique self-consciousness. Here, we follow the very emphatic statements of Ernst Käsemann.[29] It is still necessary to mark out the general historical context on the basis of which it would be understandable for Jesus to make such a claim. Here, we can refer to the apocalyptic literature. The apocalyptic visionary had a knowledge that he had obtained of events and gifts that had been shown him in advance. These were held in readiness by God for the new aeon. This knowledge constituted his claim to a proleptic-eschatological revelation, given him by God. It is also true that the recipient of such revelation is known in the apocalyptic literature only under a pseudonym, such as Enoch, Elijah, or Abraham. The concrete and unveiled ἐγώ springs the framework of what is customary in the apocalyptic tradition, and suggests additional implications. While there is no hint of an anti-Pharisaic polemic anywhere in the apocalyptic literature, there is the decisive distinction in the understanding of the Law. In distinction from the Rabbi, the consciousness of the visionary is aware of having something incomparably new and superior over and against all previous manifestations of God.[30]

At this point, two presuppositions can be seen that mark off the claims of Jesus from Rabbinic ways of thinking. First, it is only through an apocalyptic understanding of the Law that Jesus would be able to set the authority of his own "I" against the authority of the Torah as it is understood in Rabbinic theology. This means that the authority of the Torah does not appear to consist of a once-and-for-all manifestation of the will of God that can allow for all human contingencies. Rather, its authority is conceived of as an expression of the authority of the God who is active in history, and whose self-revelation in his impending eschatological activity of salvation is the goal toward which the just orient themselves in their efforts to keep the Law. The only background that would allow for the development of a polemic against the Rabbinic understanding of the Law as we find it in Jesus' teaching is a system that would direct the God-oriented gaze not toward the Law, but toward history and its end. The second point is concerned with the existence of proleptic revelation in apocalyptic theology. It is in this context where the conditions are possible for an assertion like that of Jesus, concerning his special authority quite separate from the all-encompassing authority of the Torah. These conditions exist in the diverse tradition of apocalyptic literature, which on the basis of a special divine relation teaches that this decisive final act of God already has eschatological validity over and above the Law.

Thus the structural distinction between the apocalyptic and the Rabbinic understanding of the Law, and also the apocalyptic tradition of proleptic revelation, are the two historical presuppositions for the fundamental polemic of Jesus against the Rabbinic theology.[31] The distinctions from apocalyptic thought

are significant even if we acknowledge it as the native soil for
the proclamation of Jesus, in distinction from the Rabbinic
scholastic tradition. The claims of Jesus can in no way be
sufficiently described as the "radicalization" of the claims of the
apocalyptic visionary. Not only is Lk. 10:18 the only evidence
for a visionary experience of Jesus, but also the concept of
radicalization clouds the special relationship between Jesus and
the then current apocalyptic tradition. It is better to presuppose
a completely contingent experience of Jesus as the reason for the
development of Jesus' unique claims to power. This can
best be found in the well-attested departure of Jesus from the
circle of John the Baptist. The tradition of the baptism of Jesus
is of course stamped by the post-Easter situation; but we must
take the fact that Jesus was baptized by John as a historical fact.
The Baptist had preached a final repentance in view of the
impending eschatological judgment, while Jesus for his part
had taken up the call to repentance, but also began to preach
at the same time, and with emphasis on eschatological salvation. The radical nearness of the eschatological judgment, as it
was presupposed in the preaching and conduct of the Baptist,
was transformed by Jesus into the message of the radical nearness of salvation in the inbreaking reign of God. Even within the
general framework of apocalyptic theology, the eschatology of
John the Baptist forms the immediate historical-biographical
presupposition for the eschatology of Jesus. Yet Jesus distinguishes himself from the Baptist in the immediacy with which
he claimed for himself the power of giving people a part in the
gift of eschatological salvation. Does his parting from the circle
of the Baptist (maybe after the death of John?) and
the beginning of his own activity find its reason in a special
visionary and God-inspired experience? If so, would this explain why the Christian tradition localized this experience in
Jesus' baptism in the Jordan, in that the Christian baptism
marks the beginning of the Christian-eschatological existence
in the reception of the Spirit?

All this would have to remain an unproven assertion if it could not clearly be established within the rest of the tradition about Jesus that his proclamation, in its broad outline, as well as his specific personal claim, as it came to expression in his self-consciousness, had grown up out of the tradition of concepts found in Jewish apocalyptic theology. But, since the eschatological character of the βασιλεία proclamation of Jesus has been accepted, and with it the place of this proclamation in the center of the preaching and teaching of Jesus, this stands as a proof of the apocalyptic origin and is widely accepted as such in the scholarly world. Jesus' conception of the "kingly rule of God" is different from that of the Rabbis. For them the יִהְוָה מַלְכֻּת is understood as the realization of what has come to expression in the Law. It is a dual concept for both the claim and the power of the will of God over the individual as well as the whole congregation.[32] For Jesus, the lordship of God is understood as God's eschatological act that brings the new aeon into being as the sphere of life in the presence of God, full of salvation and security. This is the imagery of apocalyptic eschatology even if the concept of the "Lordship of God" is not very common in either the apocalyptic or the Rabbinic literature. In addition, one would find the eschatological-nationalistic component that speaks of Israel's lordship over the nations. This aspect of the apocalyptic is excluded by Jesus. Jesus' usage most closely approximates that of the Jewish daily prayers. The beginning of the Kaddish prayer corresponds with the beginning of the Lord's Prayer, and one can with good reason see it as the pattern for it.[33] While the speedy coming of the rule of God is prayed for, the comparison with the language of the Lord's Prayer shows an immediacy to God which also gives a special character to the coming of the kingdom in the understanding of Jesus. The deliberately chosen address אַבָּא, rather than the most usual liturgical address of אָבְנוּ, was directly related to the eschatological event of the coming of the kingdom. When one looks at the similar expressions in the

Kaddish, then the formulation itself makes a strong impression, as though the coming of the lordship of God was a fact of such immediacy that it defined relationship between father and son in everyday categories.[34] This impression is given throughout the authentic tradition of Jesus, in the everyday conceptions in the parable of the heavenly kingdom, in the paranetic sayings to the disciples that have everyday application,[35] and also in Jesus' polemic on the Torah. That Jesus can teach with such uninhibited authority in the use of ἐγὼ δὲ λέγω ὑμῖν is also grounded in his immediacy, in which he knew the eschatological nearness of God to be around him. He is saying the same thing in the beatitude: "Blessed are the poor, for to them belongs the Kingdom of Heaven!" The authority with which he spoke of μακάριοι corresponds to the authority of the "but I say unto you" in the interpretation of the Law.

If we are to inquire after the foundation of this claim of Jesus, then we will also have to investigate the *relationship between the person of Jesus himself and the impending rule of God*. This is a difficult question to study, for in the passages where Jesus speaks of the rule of God, he says next to nothing explicitly about himself, and in the passages where he speaks about himself there is no reference to the rule of God. (We are, of course, excluding a wealth of inauthentic material at this point.) But now the apocalyptic background can help us over this difficulty. This can be clearly shown in a group of speeches, from which we will choose an example from the Q source,[36] Mt. 10:32f./Lk. 12:8f., which is in the oldest form in Luke (see Mk. 8:38/Lk. 9:26 for confirmation): "every one who acknowledges me before men, the Son of man will acknowledge before the angels of God: but who denies me before men will be denied before the angels of God." The scope of this text becomes known when one inquires into the relationship that exists between Jesus and the Son of Man. It is clear that in the earliest form spoken by Jesus, the two are distinguished from each other. It is not just a presentation of two distinct scenes, a forensic one on earth and another corresponding to it in heaven, but a presentation with two distinct personages. In the one, there is Jesus and his disciples who acknowledge or do not acknowledge Jesus, and in the other, the Son of Man who acknowledges or does not acknowledge them in heaven. However, for the rest, the relationship between these two persons remains vague. It is Matthew's account that first makes a deliberate relationship between Jesus and the Son of Man, although we can also see this as a secondary step, made possible through the post-Easter faith in the risen Jesus. It is not, however, the intention of the saying to speak about the relationship between Jesus and the Son of Man, but rather to illuminate the relationship of correspondence between the present earthly confession of the man Jesus with the heavenly-eschatological acknowledgment of his disciples by the Son of Man. The heavenly Son of Man is a more or less established figure in the apocalyptic tradition, with the function of separating the righteous from the unrighteous in connection with the final event at the end of time. It is this conception that forms the background to the second heavenly scene. The Son of Man had the final decision about who would receive salvation and who damnation. The saying says that final eschatological decision corresponds exactly with the present relationship to Jesus. This is particularly true of the descriptive force of the verbs ὁμολογεῖν and ἀρνεῖσθαι, which conceptually have nothing to do with the Son of Man, but are directed to the earthly-forensic situation and the affirmation or denial of Jesus. The relationship to Jesus—that is, the decision in the presence of men—determines the action of the Son of Man in the final judgment, which means that those related to Jesus are designated participants in the post-eschatological salvation. *The present relationship to Jesus has eschatological-soteriological (or eschatological-critical) power.* There is no stress on the temporal distinction that is presupposed throughout, namely, between Jesus' presence and the eschatological future of the Son of Man. From the standpoint of time, it does not matter how close or how far from each other these two scenes are.[37] The only point is the relationship of correspondence. Where Jesus is there, the position one takes toward him also determines what will happen at the end of time. All light is concentrated on just that earthly place where man stands present before the person of Jesus. This is the light of the eschatological event which has the character of revelation as we have been describing it. The relationship of the disciple to Jesus is the entrance to the final salvation in the new aeon. The here and now decides the future participation in salvation. The here and now decides the damnation for the rejected. Therefore: "Blessed is he who takes no offense at me" (Mt. 11:6). The call, "follow me," has the same meaning as the beatitude. The presupposition is clear: Jesus, the *person* who pronounces the blessing, is also the *place* of participation in the eschatological salvation. This sort of thing demonstrates the structure of the proleptic-eschatological revelation in apocalyptic theology. What *happened* in the company of Jesus was what the proclamation about the impending kingdom was *saying*. The disciples of Jesus, the poor, receive it here and now. And the link with the Q saying of Jesus and the Son of Man is seen even better by looking at the ending of the beatitude as it is in the oldest stage of its transmission. There at the end of the row of beatitudes is pronouncement of blessing on the one who is persecuted for Jesus' sake. The "for my sake" of the persecution in the beatitudes corresponds with the "confesses me before men" in the Son of Man saying.[38] Blessed are those who are persecuted for the sake of Jesus, because as people belonging to Jesus they are also the recipients of the eschatological salvation.[39]

With all of this similarity there still remains the apocalyptic concept of a difference between the now in the presence of Jesus and the future of the *eschaton* itself. There is the stress on the nearness of the rule of God, along with the stress on Jesus as the place of its nearness. It is decisive for the interpretation of the special eschatology of Jesus never to give up the stress on the

future of the kingdom. To be sure, there is the nearness of God's
rule as the present reality, and there is the validity of the eschatological decision concerning the person of Jesus. But, even
though it is very near at hand, the imminent future is not to be
equated with this other kind of eschatology. Within the apocalyptic framework of thought there is always that final question about the validity of the claim of Jesus, which would be
looking for verification of Jesus' claim by God. The texts show
that such a question is actually put to Jesus. In a perverted
form, it is the demand for a legitimation of Jesus through a
"sign from heaven." Jesus completely rejected this demand. It is
also just as clear that because of the attitude of Jesus, the
question remains open. The question is: To what extent is
discipleship of Jesus actually decisive about the *eschatological*
salvation? Which is only to ask in another way: In what
connection can the salvation by Jesus be acknowledged as the
eschatological act of *God*? How can it be established that Jesus
can count on such an immediacy with God, promise forgiveness
and salvation, and bring his disciples to faith in God?[40] One of
the oldest legacies of ancient Jewish apocalyptic theology is
that every divine claim will be proved true in the course of
events. We can acknowledge the truth of a declaration of God
by seeing an event of divine causation, and more than this, God
validates himself through his actions.[41] For example, the distinction between the true and false prophet is in the fulfillment
of his prophecy (Dt. 18:21f.). Later on, the claim of apocalyptic
theology to have a God-given revelation of the whole of history
also rests on the knowledge that the event at the end of time will
actually come to pass. Likewise, the whole appearance of Jesus
hangs on the final validation which God will place on his claim
at the end of history.

The miracles of Jesus ought to be understood in this same
complex of concerns. (And we must also remember that a good-
ly number of them can be judged historically probable.) This
type of reasoning can be seen in an old piece of the Q tradition

(Mt. 11:1–6). The answer of Jesus to the direct question: "Are you he who is to come, or shall we look for another?" receives the direct reply: "The blind receive their sight and the lame walk, lepers are cleansed and the deaf hear, and the dead are raised up, and the poor have the good news preached to them." All of this was expected in the course of events on the judgment day and was also taken as a sign of salvation in the new age.[42] If these miracles were done by Jesus, then they point to Jesus as "the one who is to come." This is the rationale for the answer of Jesus: "Blessed is he who takes no offense at me." Thus, these miracles are understood as the rule of God which is imminent in the company of his person, and they are therefore to be taken seriously. Likewise, we can see in the historically reliable miracle stories a reticence about burdening the stories with the extra weight of a direct eschatological legitimation of Jesus. The acts of Jesus are proofs of the new age, which cannot be directly transferred into claims about the *person* of Jesus. This kind of evidence is found in the *fate* of Jesus.

With this in mind, the attention is directed away from the appearance of Jesus in his proclamation and activity and focused on his fate. It is characteristic of the sources that they have transmitted in full detail only the final fate of Jesus in Jerusalem. According to Mark's outline, nothing prior to the final days in Jerusalem should be mentioned except a collection of various forms of tradition concerning the appearance, proclamation, teaching, controversy, and miracles of Jesus. It is only with Jesus' journey to Jerusalem that the report takes on an even quasi-biographical character and attempts to describe what really happened to Jesus. We can, of course, see a specific theological point of view coming out in this outline, but it is also clear that the traditions that were available to Mark also suppress things about Jesus out of regard for the final fate of Jesus. The nature of the tradition is such that a characterization of the life of Jesus would take the material about his journeys as strictly introductory. If something like a chronological

narration were to exist, it would not likely have much else
to report than what is presented in the first part of the Gospel
of Mark in the form of a collection of individual events. We
ought not attach too much significance to the correct assertion
of the modern critics of the gospels when they say that a biog-
raphy of Jesus would be impossible in the light of the condition
of the tradition. After all, what is essential has been handed on
to us, namely, that he spent some time going around Galilee,
until he decided to journey to Jerusalem, and that this meant a
journey to his death.

We ought to take the sources very seriously when they assert
that the death of Jesus in Jerusalem is not simply a blind plunge
but that as he made the decision to go into Jerusalem, he also
reckoned with the possibility of his death.

There is, of course, much in the material that is not historical,
as, for example, the predictions to the passion, which are post-
Easter in character. These can be seen in Mark as evidence of
literary construction. They are set into the narrative as way
stations on the road to Jerusalem. But there still is a decisive
element in the final journey to Jerusalem. We have passages
like Lk. 13:31–33 that point out that in going to Jerusalem,
Jesus was willing to reckon with the possibility of his death as
God's will for his activity. Particularly the Temple-cleansing
tradition must refer to a critical event in the court of the Temple, and from this we may decide that Jesus himself chose the
conflict. If all of this is taken in connection with his activity and
his fundamental eschatological self-understanding—and there is
little reason to doubt it—they should be viewed as arising out
of the apocalyptic world view. Jesus carried out to the extreme
his confrontation with the Pharisaic theologians in the trust that
God would prove the truth of his claim in his own fate. In
respect to the events in Jerusalem, Jesus most certainly hoped
for the eschatological act of God that would confirm his ministry
and person; for his journey to Jerusalem is not to be thought of as
an act of despair.

In the traditional range of concepts within the Jewish apocalyptic, there is evidence that there was at that time already an
acknowledgment that resurrection from the dead was an
eschatological proof. In our interpretation, it is important to
know and keep in mind that it was in just this sense that
primitive Christian faith later witnessed and understood the
resurrection. The end event has come in God's raising of Jesus
from the dead. And in that it was this Jesus, whom God had
raised up as the inbreaking of the *eschaton*, it is also true that
God had placed his stamp of approval on Jesus himself. The
resurrection of Jesus is the divine verification of the claim that
had been made in all of Jesus' behavior—especially in his pro-
nouncing of the eschatological salvation—and in all of his acts
and sayings. With this claim Jesus went directly to his death,
clearly because he had staked everything on the fact that God
would reveal him in his true eschatological reality. Although it
is so presented in the later traditions of the believing congregations, it is very unlikely that Jesus was able to plan on his own
resurrection in advance, as though it would be an isolated event
worked out by God. Equally unlikely is the supposition that
Jesus expected the general inauguration of the kingly rule of
God in connection with his own fate in Jerusalem, and combined with this the entrance into the life of the new aeon for
himself and his followers. It is evident that the witness of early
Christianity to God's eschatological resurrection was aimed at
proclaiming the final verification of the claim of Jesus through
the action of God himself. In connection with this, there was the
expectation that everyone would soon gain entrance into the
Kingdom of God. We are not thinking in conformity with
the essence or the character of the self-consciousness of Jesus,
nor in line with the primitive Christian belief in the resurrection,
when we separate the Easter event from the earthly fate of Jesus.

It is much better to draw a straight line from the claim of
Jesus to the center of the primitive Christian belief in the
resurrected one. The break that Jesus' death meant for himself

and for his disciples is an essential part of the road he had to take, for it placed his claim in total jeopardy. This expressly demonstrates that what is at stake in the fate of Jesus is the self-revelation of God. If this special claim of Jesus was somehow to be true, then it was God alone who could and must validate all Jesus stood for and prove his claim. The one who would expect verification would be one who had a relationship with Jesus like that stated in Lk. 12:8f, that is, the one who had the task of bringing about the new aeon and the participation in the eschatological salvation.

This reasoning can be shown in the history of the transmission of this text. While Jesus had made a distinction between himself and the Son of Man, the post-Easter community very soon identified the Son of Man with the risen Jesus (Mt. 10:32f.). And this is very significant from the background of apocalyptic conceptions. For when the occurrence of the resurrection of Jesus is thought of as the inauguration of the eschatological action aimed at verifying the claim of Jesus, then any distance between the now and the eschatological future disappears. If the relationship of discipleship was held onto after Easter, in the sense of this saying of Jesus, then the confession in the resurrected one is also in Jesus, who exists in the new age with God and who is the pledge to his own eschatological salvation. If Jesus is resurrected, then the end events which are now inaugurated will also concern the disciples. And since the actual gift of salvation in the *eschaton*, as seen in the apocalyptic understanding of this saying of Jesus, belongs to the figure of the Son of Man, it follows that Jesus was acknowledged as the Son of Man. The early Palestinian congregation, which lived in the same tradition of apocalyptic as Jesus, shaped a Son of Man Christology so that the experienced facts of the resurrection of Jesus were harmonized with the proclamation of Jesus. It is characteristic of this early theology to identify the past appearance of Jesus with his resurrection and present existence with God. It also makes the same kind of identification between the discipleship of the earthly Jesus and the discipleship of the risen Jesus as the Son of Man. In our perspective, this means: The first Christian theology saw and proclaimed the recent eschatological self-revelation of God to be in the appearance and fate of Jesus. In this direct connection of events, they waited for their own participation in the as the heavenly kingdom eschatological fulfillment of God's history of election.

This earliest Christian theology was nothing but an unreflective attachment to the proclamations of Jesus, projected on the brief, but still outstanding, time between the resurrection of Jesus and the universal inbreaking of the Kingdom of God. The proclamations of Jesus, the Logia, were well preserved in the tradition, and this can be observed in the sayings source that is to be judged as one of the oldest parts of the primitive tradition about Jesus.[43] While the first of the early Christian missionaries in the territory of Jewish Christendom operated under the presupposition of proclaiming the risen Jesus, they also continued to preach Jesus' own proclamation: "[Repent] The Kingdom of Heaven is at hand" (Mt. 10:7). The earliest mission proclamation that we know about has a driving compulsion to make as many as possible of the Jewish brethren into disciples of Jesus before the *eschaton*. This can be seen in Mt. 10:23: "When they persecute you in one town, flee to the next; for truly, I say to you, you will not have gone through all the towns of Israel before the Son of Man comes." What was happening in the persecutions and the conversions was understood as the last phase of the appearance of Jesus. He is now abiding in heaven while his disciples hasten around Israel carrying out his task of reaching the remnant, who can still be found for the sharing of the eschatological salvation. The congregation itself lived from day to day in expectation of the end, and with the intense consciousness of belonging to the just by virtue of the confession of Jesus, and of being the eschatological congregation of the saved.[44] Here, we can think about the liturgical expression "Maranatha," which is directed at the

risen Jesus in heaven, and which summarizes in one phrase the
expectation of the end in the primitive Palestinian congregations, together with a consciousness of the nearness of Jesus
in the very presence of the Christians: "Where two or three are
gathered in my name, there am I in the midst of them"
(Mt. 18:20). And although there are not too many passages to
prove it, it is clear that the early Palestinian congregations were
the first to possess the Spirit, who made the reality of the impending *eschaton* active and present within the congregations.
The Spirit bound the Christians of the post-Easter time together with the risen Jesus and took up the function that Jesus
had among his disciples before Easter: a function he would also
take up again when his disciples are again reunited with him
in the rule of God at the end of time.

3. THE UNDERSTANDING OF REVELATION IN THE PRE-PAULINE HELLENISTIC-CHRISTIAN MISSION TRADITION AND IN PAUL

The Hellenistic-Christian sphere of tradition, which is known
to us primarily through the witness of Paul, has a character
that is essentially determined by its origin. The Christian
congregations in Greek-speaking Asia Minor had sprung up
through a fast and far-reaching mission whose course and character were decisively determined by one man, Paul. His proclamation was greatly influenced by the kerygmatic state of the
tradition in nearby Syria, which was also oriented to mission,
both before and after the time of Paul. We know very little
of how this Syrian-Gentile Christianity had arisen. The standing
conflicts between Antioch and Jerusalem would indicate that
these Gentile Christians could hardly credit their origin to the
exclusively Jewish-oriented Jerusalem mission. Moreover, the
kerygmatic tradition that can be found in the Pauline and deutero-Pauline writings is so strikingly different from the Jerusalem tradition (which determined the life, faith, and mission
of the first Jewish Christian congregations) that it cannot be

seen as arising directly out of this either. Nevertheless, there is a connecting link between the Gentile and the Jewish Christians, a common central point of departure for all theological thought and life. This is the knowledge of the resurrection of Jesus as the decisive beginning of the final event—a very important finding from the point of tradition history. The pre-Pauline Gentile Christian tradition has its center in the resurrection faith of Jewish apocalyptic, which links it with the primitive community. Thus, both communities have theologies with a common heritage as points of departure, namely, the *heilsgeschichtliche* frame of reference coming from Jewish apocalyptic. Before he was converted, Paul was obviously a Jewish theologian in the apocalyptic tradition.[45] This early aspect of his life retained its decisive influence on him in the development of his own thinking as a Christian theologian and only served to strengthen a tendency already at work in Gentile Christianity from its very inception.

The proclamation that Paul carried to the congregations established by him, and that is clearly in agreement with that of Gentile Christian missionaries, has a common stock of material that could be summarized in the following manner: (1) In contrast to the many deities of Hellenistic syncretism stands the God of the (Jewish) history of election, who is the one true God, and who is creator and Lord of all. (2) As such, God will very shortly execute a universal judgment of all men, and in view of this, men ought to turn to him. (3) The conversion to this God is brought about by faith in Jesus as the one whom God has raised from the dead and appointed Lord of all (κύριος πάντων), for the resurrection of Jesus is the beginning of the final act of God, which is close at hand. (4) The ascended Jesus will very shortly descend from heaven as the savior of the believers, both Jew and Gentile. (Both the Jewish and Gentile unbelievers will fall victim to an eternal destruction.)[46] If we compare the schema of this preaching with the first Jewish Christian tradition, the common apocalyptic framework is easily perceived. This aspect of the central tradition of Gentile Christianity is further strengthened by the adoption of the tradition of proof-texting, so that the manner of expression in the Greek Bible made a deep impression on the thinking of the Hellenistic Christian. Finally, the adoption of the *heilsgeschicht-liche* self-designation of the Christian by reference to the ἐκκλησία τοῦ θεοῦ served the same purpose in the language of the Hellenistic Christian. The Hellenistic community stood together with the Jerusalem congregation and made a common front against the Jewish community in claiming that they were the true congregation of God.

Although there is a striking reduction in attention to the final destiny of Jesus, it is also true for the Gentile Christian tradition that it saw the beginning of the eschatological self-revelation in Jesus in much the same way that apocalyptic theology expected it in the end events. The past of Jesus' fate, his death, and his resurrection were viewed in a somewhat unreflected manner as a unity with the present and the anticipated future. The expression of this was chiefly the many-sided experience of the Spirit, which had become one of the leading manifestations of the whole of the contemporary Christian life (Jewish and Hellenistic alike). The manifold spiritual *charismata* were held to be the experience and the expression of the imminent higher world of God's salvation. The activity of the Spirit and the activity of the risen and ascended Jesus as the heavenly *Kurios* were seen as interlocking activities, without much distinction in function, yet without being thereby identical either. And thus, the present experience of the Spirit, which was the universal determining element in the daily life and, even more, the worship life of Hellenistic Christianity, was taken to be a uniquely experiential proof of the *heilsgeschichtliche* interconnection between the fate of Jesus, the present, and the future *eschaton*, as a unique connection of cosmic events in which God is about to reveal the end of time as the one culminating event of the whole process of God's revelation.

In the first place, all of this is just as valid for Paul himself. This must be understood if we are to comprehend the particular theological decision and its direction as Paul inherited it in connection with his mission activity.

It was not only something like the above-described kerygma that he brought to the newly established congregations, but also the reality of belonging to Christ that meant being grasped by the Spirit.[47] In fact, the event of coming to faith and the reception of the Spirit mark out one singular context of experience. However, such faith is not fundamentally understood as the fruit of the Spirit, for faith is rather comprehended as a trusting in God on the basis of the kerygma, which means trusting in Jesus, whom God had raised from the dead.[48] However, the possibility of such faith is what is understood as a gift of God. If Paul can use πίστις in the sense of the end epoch in the *Heilsgeschichte* (e.g., Gal. 3:23), this general understanding will also color such theological expressions—ἐκ πίστεως that means κατὰ χάριν (Rom. 4:16). In a discussion of the gifts of the Spirit (Rom. 12:3), Paul can say that God has given to each man his own measure of faith. This can only be understood when we keep in mind the basic agreement of Paul with the Christian experience of faith that was going on around him, which was directed toward the Christ event, and seen together with the present experience of the Spirit. The freedom from Law, sin, and death, which is fundamentally constituted as an act of God brought about through the event of Christ (Rom. 8:3f.), can also be presented in the same context as something constituted by the Law of the Spirit (Rom. 8:2). In the same way, the present situation of the free man can so be described that Christ (Rom. 8:10), and also at the same time the Spirit (Rom. 8:11), lives in the Christian. For the Spirit is the Spirit of him who raised Jesus from the dead and who therefore (in the perspective of Easter) can also be designated as the πνεῦμα Χριστοῦ (Rom. 8:9). Thus, we finally come to this conclusion: In Paul, the ascended Jesus is often spoken of as the *Kurios* and

as the presently experienced Spirit in such a way that they seem
to be treated in parallel without much distinction being made;
yet, at the same time, Paul does not make an out-and-out
identification of the ascended Lord with the Spirit.[49]

As long as these expressions had their horizon focused on the
fundamental complex of apocalyptic concepts, Paul was not
obligated to make theological-critical distinctions in the living
tradition. He simply lived in this stream of tradition and took a
leading part in its spread. However, he was obligated to make
a theological judgment in a particular situation. There was a
movement in the Corinthian congregation that not only wished
to get out from under the authority of Paul, but which wished
to press for radical changes in the practice of the life of the congregation based on a gnostic interpretation of the Christian
tradition. As Paul had perceived in his discussion, the center of
the Christian tradition was decisively altered in this movement.
It was here that the eschatological exuberance of the contemporary pneuma-experience flowed into gnostic-formed ways of
thinking and left the original channels of the Jewish apocalyptic
theology. The ascended Lord and the Spirit were here consciously identified. The tradition about the fate of Jesus was altered into a gnostic redeemer myth. The present experience of
the Spirit was interpreted as the identification of the Christian
with the ascended Christ. The whole concept of the future was
swallowed up in the here and now of the pneumatic existence,
and thus it was consciously corrupted. But most of all, the past
earthly life of Jesus was declared meaningless for the "perfected"
pneumatic.[50]

This situation was not to be judged as a sudden apostasy of
the Corinthian congregation to a "heresy" that had come in
from the outside. It was rather the natural development of a
congregation which was composed of men who were largely
Christianized out of the Hellenistic-gnostic background. However, for the discerning eye of Paul, it was evident that a fundamental problem was beginning to develop in the Christian

tradition among the non-Jewish Hellenistic Christians, which called for a clear solution. Sharply stated, the question was: What is to be acknowledged as *the* divine and decisively saving eschatological act of revelation? Is it the past fate of Jesus, *or* the present experience of the Spirit, *or* the imminent future of the parousia of the ascended one? The tradition had affirmed these to be one unified happening. Paul also had this same point of view, and therefore he did not see the fundamental problem with the sharpness we have expressed nor did he allow the solution of the problem in Corinth to break the horizons of this tradition. While his antithesis against the gnostic position of the Corinthians always remained within the traditional horizons, from the beginning it nevertheless modified the previous profile of the Hellentistic Christian tradition history. This tradition saw the outlines of the imminent future in the present experience of the Spirit. From this point of view, the Corinthian position would have been simply one more step beyond Paul in this direction, if they had not been so provocatively formulated.

In opposing this, Paul insisted on the acknowledgment of three assertions with all the passion and uncompromising energy he could muster.

Assertion number one: All the salvation of the Christian is dependent on what came to pass in the past fate of Jesus. Faith is oriented to the past occurrence of the resurrection of Jesus by God. The ascended one is also the crucified one. As the Christian looks to the Lord on high, he should not for one moment divert his gaze from the past events of his earthly fate.

Assertion number two: The future realization of eschatological participation in salvation cannot be eliminated. With this there is given a distinction between Christ and the Christian that ought not be bridged in eschatological enthusiasm. Through God's eschatological act, the once-crucified Jesus was perfected in his resurrection as a single person and as "the first fruits of those who have fallen asleep" (I Cor. 15:20, 23). Because of this, the Christian resurrection is always an impending one until the end event encompasses the whole cosmos. In connection with the parousia of their ascended Lord, the Christians will be led into the life of the new age and the glory of God. Indeed, all this *will* happen because Christ *died for them* and was raised, once and for all.[51] Therefore, the present for the Christian is first defined only on the basis of the participation in the fate of Jesus on the cross and not in the Corinthian sense of a pneumatic and immediate possession of salvation ("Christ crucified," I Cor. 1:18). Holding the future in reserve to oppose the gnostic tendency, which radically contemporized the eschatological future, meant that Paul was holding to the *heilsgeschichtliche* central character of Christ's death *for us* as an action of *grace*. Christ has died for us, and we all have a share in his death (II. Cor. 5:14, etc.). The one who had died for us has been raised by God, and our present participation in the fate of his death is also a perfect liberation from the Law, sin, and death. As we do not yet participate in the resurrection of Christ, and as we will only participate through our own resurrection in the future end event, there is, at present, a distinction between Christ and us. This eschatological distance holds in reserve the "for us" of the past event of Christ as a happening of God's grace, which has salvatory validity for the present time of the Christian in an eschatological way. Therefore the gracious character of the salvation event in Christ is grounded in the faith based on the past event of Christ as God's act of salvation. This is also continually and essentially bound up with the hope and also orients itself to the impending eschatological act of God for the Christian.[52]

Finally, assertion number three: The authority of the apostle is not legitimated through manifestations of Spirit-possession, but rather in his having seen the ascended Christ in a proleptic "revelation" given by God, and also in his mission to proclaim the crucified Christ.[53]

Thus, Paul energetically guarded the apocalyptic foundations of the primitive Christian tradition in opposition to the gnostic position. While the past, present, and future were certainly bound closely together into one complex of eschatological action, this traditional understanding nevertheless experienced a certain qualification as a result of Paul's confrontation with the Hellenistic Corinthians. His sharply delineated difference between Christ and the Christian implied a distinction between the past of the Christ event, the present of the Christians, and the future of their participation in the salvation. His sharply polemic proclamation of the crucified Christ made clear both the past character of the Christ event and also its historical distance from the now of the believer. The defense of the traditional expression about the future against the gnostic *nunc aeternum* also made clear the gap between the expected future and the here and now of the believing and hoping ones. Paul emphatically held on to the experience of the Spirit in the tradition, through which future, present, and past actually seemed at times to eschatologically coincide. This was a necessary bridge in his theology, but it was also a usable argument in his polemic against the gnostic position. The point is, when the polemic accent on the historical distance between Christ and the Christian presses for a theological acknowledgement of *history*, which extends to Christians in past, present, and future, then the expressions about the Spirit have a counterbalancing effect. From our vantage point, it is clear that throughout the whole of Pauline theology there was a tension of unbalanced tendencies, which, if they are to be judged in historical perspective, represent nothing more than a theological-critical sharpening of a tension that was implicit from the very beginning of the primitive Christian tradition. In the last analysis, it is grounded in the unique self-consciousness of Jesus and in the divine endorsement given him in the resurrection. His relationship to the continuing but now "Christian" history was not clarified, but it demanded clarification if the reality of the soteriological power of the fate of Jesus was to be asserted in a continually convincing fashion.

Because of lack of space, I must here curtail the presentation of the second confrontation of Paul and its significance. This was against the Judaizers, who fought against the equal validity of Gentile Christianity in the history of salvation by their demands for circumcision.[54] At this point it must be shown how the apocalyptically defined framework of the Hellenistic Christian tradition was placed in question by a controversy that this time came out of the Jewish side of things. In Paul's theological judgment, to demand a universal applicability of the Law to all Christians would nullify the *heilsgeschichtliche* universality of the Christ event as the eschatological revelation of God, and this would have meant that "Christ died to no purpose" (Gal. 2:21). Finally, the last extant witness of Paul, his Letter to the Romans, shows the position that he had worked out in the Corinthian-gnostic troubles. It also shows with even more clarity the theological judgment that was pronounced in the anti-Judaistic confrontation in Galatia. We conclude by observing that—taken in connection with a framework of *Heilsgeschichte*, and on the basis of the *heilsgeschichtliche* function of the Christ event as the eschatological-universal revelation of God for Jews and Gentiles—the doctrine of justification in the Letter to the Romans is in fact the "summa" of Paul's theology, and for that matter, of his life.

4. THE UNDERSTANDING OF REVELATION IN MARK AND LUKE

With the exception of a few logia in paranetic contexts, Paul took over no Jesus tradition of a synoptic kind. Even in his strong concentration on what took place in the past, his theology is centered on the fate of Jesus, not his manner of life, his proclamation and activity.[55] The same impression can be obtained from the sphere of tradition that surrounds Paul (Ephesians, Colossians, and also I Peter and the pastorals, in the sense of showing very different beginnings in the attempt to picture the earthly Jesus as an example for Christians). In the first decades of its development, Gentile Christianity of Asia Minor exhibited no knowledge of any image of the historical Jesus. The history of the synoptic tradition seems to have run a parallel course to the kerygmatic tradition of Paul's missionary congregations with almost no connection.

However, while the synoptic tradition had its beginning stage of development in the early congregations of Jewish Christianity, it very quickly shifted over to the Hellenistic community, in which its character was changed to a very marked degree. In this new environment, Jesus appeared very much like a divine being (Θεῖος ἀνήρ) who had descended from heaven in human form as a savior of the sick and the poor, master of the demonic powers, and revealer of the hidden secrets of God. The apocalyptic concepts, which were part of the background of the Jewish Christian tradition of Jesus, were more and more overshadowed by this Hellenist image. This is especially true for Jesus' claims to revelation, which were altered into the fundamental concept of a powerful and brilliant epiphany of the divine on earth in the extraordinary form of Jesus.

The evangelist Mark made the first attempt to combine the rapidly expanding and diverse tradition of Jesus into a unified presentation and also to connect this with the primitive mission kerygma, which had in the meantime become normative in the far-flung reaches of Hellenistic Christianity. Because of this, his work is of extreme significance for understanding the history of tradition. The few simple facts of this collection into the first written "gospel" are as follows: Mark created the *outline* for the arrangement of the material that had a definitive influence on the later history of the tradition, as can be seen in the gospels of Matthew and Luke, which are independent of each other, and yet rely on Mark. The Gospel of Mark begins with the appearance of the Baptist. This in turn makes the appearance of Jesus more impressive. As the material from the tradition expressed it, with Jesus, the Son of God has come on earth. In the rest of the work, the remarkable acts of power done by this Son of

God are presented in simple succession, with all the diversity of narrative that can be found in the Jewish Christian, and Hellenistic Christian traditions. However, Mark has thrown the veil of the so-called Messianic secret over this material. Who he is can be seen in the continual demonstration of his epiphany in the miracle stories; nevertheless, this knowledge remains hidden from the men of that time. After the revelation of Jesus at his baptism, the confession of Peter at Caesarea Philippi is the first express confession about the true being of Jesus. This confession of Peter serves the evangelist in a literary way, so from here on everything that follows points to the passion in Jerusalem. Of course, from time to time there are individual reminders of who Jesus is, but for the rest the reader is to know this and read the unfolding passion story in this light. But where did the reader get this idea? The purpose in Mark's conception for placing the veil of the Messianic secret over an entire tradition that was epiphany in form was to make the Jesus tradition as a totality into an epiphany for the benefit of the post-Easter Christians. Exactly who Jesus was was first recognized after the resurrection (Mk. 9:9). Thus, the contemporary baptismal confession, in which Jesus was acknowledged as the "Son of God," was the completed profession concerning the essence of Jesus. The veil that surrounds the figure of the earthly Jesus in the presentation of Mark was oriented to the end, namely, the passion and the resurrection, just as the three predictions to the passion were. Before Easter Jesus could be experienced only in a veiled way, but *now*—in the Christian's own present time—believers can experience the confrontation with the Risen One in an unveiled way. Thus Mark also put all of the material about Jesus that had been transmitted to him, into the profile of the Hellenistic Christian kerygmatic tradition. As we have seen, this tradition aimed at making the ascended Lord known. He was the one who was in heaven with God, standing ready to come down and gather in the elect, because the final catastrophe was breaking in on the world (see Mk. 13:24ff.), but who was also already here and now known as a present epiphany in his congregations. Mark had explicitly mentioned the total kerygmatic understanding of his gospel in the title (Mk. 1:1). His book was a presentation of his collection of the Jesus material, and he called it "The Gospel of Jesus Christ."[56] But in this way the Gospel of Mark is nothing other than a noteworthy witness to that Hellenistic theological situation that we already have become quite well acquainted with as the thought world of Paul. Here, of course, it was with the assimilation of the tradition of Jesus. We also see in Mark that there is no consciousness of the problem that arises in the distinction between the past of Jesus and the present of the Christians. With regard to the distinction between the present of the Christian and his future, we can see the first traces of the consciousness of the so-called delay of the parousia.[57] Mark's accomplishment was in fashioning a sensitive response to the theological situation of his environment in the first ordering of the many-sided material in the tradition.

In contrast, the work of Luke, judged as a whole, is a good step beyond Mark. While Mark had shaped the first gospel, it was Luke who wrote the first church history as a continuation of his gospel. This double book of Luke was something new in the history of transmission. There was nothing like it again for a long time, and it shows the impressive contribution of this theologian of the second Christian generation. He had seen the problem in the whole of the primitive Christian tradition and set forth a solution that had amazing theological consequences and that was bound to an important literary destiny.

Already the editing of the Marcan original in his gospel constantly shows the hand of the critical theologian,[58] although the Marcan tradition on which he was working still had the upper hand because of its own impressiveness as a total work. The specific Lucan theology can be recognized much more clearly in the Book of Acts, in which Luke is dependent on individual sources alone, but not on any outline of the total plan of the work. This is especially true in the mission sermons of the apostles, which are an important element in the structure of the work and which are as good as totally shaped by Luke himself.[59]

On the one hand, Luke assumes that all of what is transmitted in the tradition of Jesus (about the deeds and the proclamation, as well as his fate) is a *past occurrence* from which the Christians of his generation are irretrievably separated. The historical distance from the earthly Jesus is known in its full weight, and is theologically mastered. On the other hand, the consciousness of the historical progression of time must also concern the future *eschaton* and emphasize its distance from the Christian's own present. In view of the drawing apart of past, present, and future, which was based on the historical experience of the second generation, there was a sharpening of the question of the historical place given the decisively salvatory, single revelation of God. Interestingly enough, this was a question for the critical eye of the theologian of this second generation, which was matched by only one person before him, namely, Paul. Where is the Christian at the close of the first century to find his salvation—in the past *or* in the future, *or* in his own present? All of this was asked in view of the gradually expanding primitive Christian eschatological understanding of the post-Easter present, an understanding that is expanded in view of the simple reality of experienced history in the interim. Apparently without any personal knowledge of Pauline theology, Luke had answered the question along the same line as Paul did in the conflict with the Corinthian gnostics. As the problematic of the eschatological character of the primitive Christian tradition becomes clear to the members of the second generation, their own solution becomes radical. *The* eschatological salvation for the presently living Christian had been worked by the past event of Jesus. Insofar as Luke, in a sharper way than the many-sided tradition before him, had presented all the action and conduct of Jesus as the salvation-producing action *of God*— coming to final fruition in the resurrection of Jesus as the action of God that brings together all the past activity of salvation— he had in this way given to the Jesus event the full dignity of what was proclaimed in the apocalyptic primitive Christian tradition as the *eschatological* revelation of God. It was now necessary to reserve the specifically eschatological concepts of the tradition to the *eschaton*, which is still to be expected in the future that is now removed into the indefinable historical distance. Luke himself was not at home in apocalyptic thinking, but he was in the position to distinguish sharply the content of primitive Christian apocalyptic thinking from the eschatological imagery within this tradition; to center the content on the event of Jesus, and to leave the imagery to the eschatological future. The imagery had lost content and consequently could hardly be considered as events that had decisive significance for salvation. Salvation has been completed. Salvation was present among men in Jesus of Nazareth; that is, in his healing and exorcistic miracles, God inaugurated a temporal sphere of active and manifest salvation on earth. The Jewish hostility could not prevail against this salvation of God in Jesus of Nazareth. These people were able to kill Jesus, but in this, the demonstrable injustice of their actions became evident to right-minded men of all ages. From his point of view, God made the crime of the Jews to no effect through the act of resurrecting Jesus, and therefore there are witnesses, the apostles, who have a common experience of the whole history of Jesus including the forty-day association with the bodily resurrected one.

The history of Jesus as a historical time is closed with the ascension, and with this, the unmediated presence of salvation on earth. With the exception of a few interventions of the Ascended One into the destiny of his earthly congregation, there is no longer any unmediated-actual participation in salvation for the post-Easter Christianity, nor any confrontation with Jesus. Since his ascension, Jesus can be found at the right hand of God, from whence he will descend again only in connection with the final event, and will again bring back to earth the unmediated presence of his salvation. This was, of course, what his presence on earth meant for his disciples. Even the Spirit does not bestow salvation in an unmediated-actual way, but in a mediated way, which means that the Spirit has come down from heaven and is constantly working in his congregations, supporting the apostolic proclamation of the salvation of all men that has come about through the event of Jesus.[60] There is a present salvation only in the "name" Jesus of Nazareth (Acts 4:12), namely, what the apostolic witness said about Jesus. And such salvation, constituted by God in the past event of Jesus and mediated to us in proclamation, is at the same time a total salvation that accomplishes present forgiveness of sins for those who have repented.

And how is the guarantee of salvation in this past event of Jesus made real for the Christian of the present? It is very noteworthy that a direct answer to this is not found in the Lucan writings. But it would sound something like this in the meaning of Luke: Salvation is the history of Jesus in that these events have actually happened as *Acts of God*. This makes explicit the theory of *Heilsgeschichte*, in which Luke sought to place anew the real concerns of an apocalyptic theology of history in a manner that is strange to apocalyptic theology itself.[61] All history before Jesus had proleptic character, that is, it was ordered from the very beginning in God's plan of history, which pointed to the history of Jesus as "fulfillment," the decisively salvatory "middle of time."[62] All history following on this history of Jesus is by definition *the time of historical participation in salvation*, on the basis of the "fulfilled" time, which is not in the past. That is Luke's meaning of church history, whose course is sketched out in the second half of his double work. In a quick succession of victories during the time after Easter, the whole world received the proclamation of the history of Jesus. It began in the little town of Jerusalem, the place where Jesus ended his ministry, and extended to wider circles. The first barrier to fall was the one between Jew and Gentile. In Acts one can read of Paul, who is treated less like an apostle and more like a church missionary of the postapostolic period, carrying the proclamation of salvation (which was historically mediated) into the whole of the eastern half of the Empire, and finally to Rome. This all happened according to God's plan, just as all *Heilsgeschichte* is fulfilled according to his plan. Thus, church history, as the history of the apostolic proclamation of Jesus, is an explication, in historical and epic form, of the fulfillment of the past event of Jesus in its universal validity.

Then, someday, the end will come with the cosmic catastrophe and the judgment of the living and the dead. But this end will not bring anything new with respect to salvation, nor will it question anything that has been established. Thus, the end will be the salvation accomplished by the history of Jesus, that is, Jesus will be brought back in person. We can picture the ascended Jesus descending from heaven exactly as he was when the apostles saw him ascend (Acts 1:11). It is not fitting for Christians to know when this would be—whether "in this time" or later—for the soteriology had become fully independent of the traditional eschatology. In a radical way Luke had set the soteriological elements of traditional eschatology into the history of the realized plan of God. One of the most appropriate ways to characterize the theology of Luke would be by the title of this book of essays, *Revelation as History*.

However, we should qualify this conclusion because there is a final point of unclarity in the Lucan solution. We can rightly ask Luke: "How is the history of Jesus *salvatory* for the present believer? How could the Jesus of *time past* be my salvation in time present?" To this he would answer: "Because the history of Jesus was *God's* act." But we cannot ask Luke: "How would the act of *God* in past time become an act of salvation?"; then Luke would have nothing to say, for he would have been asked too much, and no clear answer can be found in his work. From the point of view of the history of tradition this is connected with the fact that the Pauline soteriological expressions

(the death of Jesus ὑπὲρ ἡμῶν) are missing. In addition there is
the factor of the history of culture. The *Heilsgeschichte* of Luke
is that of a Hellenistic historian rather than that of an apocalyptic theologian. The question regarding the foundation of
salvation in view of the acts of God is a question that was too
big for the static character of the Lucan conception of *Heilsgeschichte* as a closed, well-organized system of events.[63]

5. The Understanding of Revelation in the Letter to the Hebrews

It is astonishing to note how the second generation proposed
so many different answers to the problems that it had received
from the primitive Christian tradition of the first generation.
Along with Luke, we will here mention the author of Hebrews,
whose work is perhaps the first direct witness we have to Egyptian Christianity.

It is possible to obtain an insight into the perspective of the
author of Hebrews by seeing the baptismal confession of
the ascended Son of God as the key to the interpretation of the
epistle.[64] This confession spoke of the exaltation of the Son as
the high priest into the heavenly Holy of Holies. In this action,
the dead pass through death and beyond to be on high with
God. It is the course of salvation out of the "flesh" into the
higher sphere of life intended for Christians (esp. 10:19).
The hymnlike sentences with which the author introduced his
letter (1:2f.) contain this confession. The manifold ways in
which God spoke through the prophets have "in these last days"
come to their conclusion and goal through the speaking of God
in his Son, through the Son's exaltation to the right hand of the
majesty of God, where he has brought about cleansing from
sins. This basic expression interprets the total letter. The heavenly enthronement of the Exalted One is then expounded (1:5ff.).
From there, the attention is directed on the earthly event,
through which the decisively salvatory beginning of the office of

the heavenly high priest is prepared. The exaltation followed hard upon the humiliation of the Son in the sharing of the flesh and blood of his brothers on the earth below. As the ἀρχηγὸς τῆς σωτηρίας of these people, he will be glorified because of the suffering, in that he had to pass through it and therefore maintain his fellowship with men to the very last, so that he became a faithful high priest and Mediator before God in heaven (2:5–18). And thus, by passing through the heavens, he entered into the sanctuary on high, where he offered himself, as the eternal priest, to God as the perfect "once and for all" sacrifice. He became like his brothers on earth in all respects, excepting the fact he was without sin (4:15). He learned perfect obedience through what he had to suffer in "loud cries and tears" (5:7), and he was therefore proved worthy and established by God as the glorified and "perfect" high priest who was to become the source of eternal salvation for his own on earth (5:8).[65]

From here it follows that everyone who now obeys him (5:8) and holds fast to his confession (4:14) is in a great pilgrimage with the faithful of all ages (ch. 11) and is going on the way that he had traversed before them as the "pioneer and perfector of our faith." This means that he had opened the way to salvation through his ascent and the offering of himself. The faithful still see this goal in hope: Faith is hope (11:1). Their hope is anchored in Christ, their high priest, who has been established on high, where he carries on an eternal intercession for them in the heavenly Holy of Holies (6:16 ff.), which is also the goal they are approaching in their pilgrimage. This journey to the salvation on high corresponds to, and also exceeds, the wandering of the Israelites under the leadership of Moses. As the people of old approached the earthly Sinai, the true believers march on in hope to Zion on high, the worshiping congregation in the heavenly Jerusalem composed of the sons made perfect through God's proclamation of judgment (12:18ff.).

When the goal of the pilgrimage of faith is finally reached,

then the things made possible "in the last times" through the
way of Christ as the high priest (Jesus Christ who is the same
yesterday, today, and forever, 13:8) "will appear a second
time" to those who are now awaiting his coming (9:28).
This is an appearance "for salvation" and will be the perfection
of the saints, brought about in his perfection. This "second
coming" will not be a repetition of his first, which was one of
condescension, but a coming of the exalted high priest in
which he does not become like them, but they like him. Just
as the first advent in suffering proceeds on the assumption that
the one person could become the eternal high priest of the
many as their "brother" (2:10ff.), so also his future second
coming "perfects" the cultic "sanctification" of the many in
their being brought into the sanctuary on high.[66] Just as the
christological event has found its goal and perfection in heaven,
the *soteriological* event will also be perfected in heaven. The
perfection is redemption from the constriction of the earthly.

Ernst Käsemann was the first to see the implication for the
history of religion by judging this to be an interesting apoca-
lyptic-primitive Christian tradition translated into a gnostic
framework.[67] The item to be stressed for our discussion is this—
the writer of Hebrews is like Luke in distinguishing between
past, present, and future (see again 13:8) and also between
Jesus on the one hand and the Christian on the other. However,
in contrast to Luke, he has located the place of salvation in
heaven, which means the eschatological future, so far as the
present Christian is concerned. Herein we can recognize his
own theological decision. Especially in view of the strongly
gnostic character of this thought, it is striking that the writer
has located the reception of salvation so decisively *in the eschatological future.* The primitive Christian tradition interpreted
along gnostic lines was the direct heritage of the author of
Hebrews. Probably his gnostic Christian environment had
taken over the primitive Christian eschatological tradition—
similar to the prologue of I Peter—and reinterpreted it in

gnostic terms in the way the congregation in Corinth had done. In view of this, it is even more astounding that he has executed this totally ungnostic turn to the future, and has sought in this manner to protect the primitive Christian tradition and interpreted it anew in its entirety. This could have been because he—as Luke—recognized the problem of content and form in eschatological tradition, and at the same time the deep alienation of its gnostic reinterpretation. However, in distinction from Luke, he saw the solution in the exclusive concentration of all expressions of salvation on the heavenly future. Such a solution as that of Luke's was out of the question for him in his historical situation, because, with the exception of the passion account, he had very little access to the traditions about Jesus that were known to Luke. In this respect, the writer of Hebrews was in a situation like that of Paul. In general, it would not dawn on a Christian such as this man, who had grown up in the gnostic tradition, that a past event could be salvatory in its pastness. The structure of *heilsgeschichtliche* thought is totally strange to a gnostic. In the primitive Christian tradition, the distinction between Christ and the Christian was an essential distinction. Within the gnostic framework this distinction was only conceivable as a distance between a nonsalvatory present and its future triumph, and this causes his Christology to run the danger—as everywhere in gnostic thought—of turning into a mythological image of the soteriological process. This could be avoided when the pastness of the fate of Jesus is acknowledged as an accomplished salvation and thought through theologically. This possibility of thought was closed to the writer of Hebrews by his own historical situation.

6. The Understanding of Revelation in the Gospel of John

There is yet another theologically critical solution of this same problem distinct from that of Luke and the writer of

Hebrews. This was blocked out by the fourth evangelist within his own situation in the history of tradition. No matter how difficult this matter may be, it is more and more evident that the background of the Gospel of John is an oriental-gnostic Christianity. This is possible in the east-Jordanian, inner-Syrian section of the church, which came into being out of the Jewish Christian sphere of the primitive Christian tradition, but was not influenced by the pre-Pauline, pre-Syrian, Hellenistic mission kerygma.[68] The Gospel of Mark—and one or both of the other synoptic gospels—was not known to the fourth evangelist. Whether he had another written gospel before him or whether he had taken his material primarily out of the oral tradition is not yet sufficiently clarified. In our discussion, the more important task is to understand the theological character of the pre-Johannine tradition.

The miracle stories of the first part have a totally un-Jewish atmosphere in spite of the Jewish coloration. Jesus is here characterized as the Θεῖος ἀνήρ. This is dominated by a spirit similar to that of the Gospel of Mark. From the beginning to the climax in the raising of the dead in chapter eleven, Jesus' healings and miracles are described as an epiphany-like documentation of the divine glory. His omniscience, which he uses to see through those who come to him, is proof of his divine nature. Thus, in Jesus, a divine being is on the earth among men. He is the Logos, who was in the beginning with God, and who became flesh; who was the one who made the divine glory visible on earth in his person.[69] He is the "Son of Man" who has descended from heaven in order to give the world the true, divine life, and then to again ascend into heaven. And thus Jesus' time on earth is presented as a whole in which the manifestations of glory have come out of the higher world in the person of the divine bringer of salvation who has descended in the flesh as man among men. Everything points to this, that in the pre-Johannine tradition this heavenly brilliance of Jesus was still felt to permeate the Christian presence. The same is proved by the gnostic character of the Johannine image of Christ. Similar to the later Mandaean literature and especially like the almost contemporary Odes of Solomon, the fulness of salvation through the person of the Revealer-Redeemer, in his very being on earth, is considered to be the possibility of knowing the divine. In the possession of this knowledge, man can already be freed from the imprisonment of the world. To be sure, the background of this pre-Johannine Christian gnosis is the Jewish Christian tradition, whose conceptuality has in part been retained in this foreign climate. An example of this would be the eschatological conception of the judgment that God has given over to Jesus as the Son of Man and also of the future resurrection of the dead. These eschatological pictures may have led their own independent life alongside those features in the picture of Jesus that aim at the experience of his epiphany in the present. All of this can exist together only in a very diverse congregational tradition. The situation here is fundamentally like that of the rest of primitive Christianity: the tradition of the early church was not uniform.

Thus, in his own situation, the fourth evangelist attempted a radical solution to the problem of the tension between past, present, and future. He reacted in his situation much like Luke or the writer of Hebrew in his. His solution is to be understood in the plan of his gospel.

The first part of the gospel shows Jesus as the divine Logos who has come upon the earth and appeared in the flesh. This is how he is praised in the hymn that the writer took over from the cult of his congregation and used as the prologue of his gospel. All interest is concentrated on the person of this unusual divine man, who was sent from the heavenly Father so that his glory is manifest in this person (1:14; compare 2:11), and men can see the Father himself in seeing him and acknowledging him as the one sent by the Father. In the context of Johannine theology, the act of belief is to go to Jesus in person, see him in his essence as the revealer of the Father, and remain

with him as his disciple.[70] The miracles as well as the speeches
serve to establish the confession of faith. They are signs,
especially 2:11. This is also the theological meaning of the frequent linking of miracle and speech of revelation in one unified
pericope. The evangelist does everything to concentrate the view
on Jesus with the radical consequent meaning. In this Jesus, as the
one sent by the Father, is the full, unsurpassed revelation; and
in the faith of the disciples in Jesus, the reality of this full and
unsurpassed salvation has become earthbound experiential
reality. As a result, the evangelist engages in an obvious polemic
against the traditional elements of an eschatological expectation of judgment and salvation by transferring all the expectations of the future wholly on the presence of Jesus. In his
earthly mission, Jesus himself carried out the eschatological
judgment in that the believing and the unbelieving distinguish themselves in their relation to his person. The believers
have eternal life through their faith; the unbelievers, in contrast,
are already judged, precisely because they do not believe in
Jesus (e.g., 3:18, 36; 5:24). And the signs of Jesus point out this
same fact—the presence and power of the eschatologically
expected glory of God in the one who is sent by God. From this
perspective, the miracles of Jesus have an apparently symbolic
character. The healing of the man born blind "symbolizes" the
noncomprehending world and its act of coming to faith in the
dark of the night (9:39; compare 8:12; 12:35f.). The raising
of Lazarus is the documentation of the reality of Jesus' claim
to be the personification of the resurrection and the life (11:25;
compare 5:24). However, this common linkage of the event of
miracle and the event of faith ought not in reality be given a
symbolic sense as though the miracles were regarded as coded
messages in the understanding of Jesus, which could only be
understood in the light of the speeches of Jesus attached to them.

Rather, the miracle stories ought to anchor the mind of the
reader back on the event of the miracle, which is to be studied
as the constant background of the revelatory speeches of Jesus.

Both belong together as events in the past. The salvation on earth was confrontable as an earthly phenomenon in Jesus, the σάρξ γενόμενος, that faith means to approach Jesus, see him, and follow him. It is in just such a visibly demonstrative way that the miracles of Jesus are proof of who he is.[71] The miracles are signs for faith insofar as the believer who sees these signs of Jesus perceives in them the reality of his true understanding of Jesus. This is the meaning of the apparent symbolic link between the event of the miracle and the event of faith. But naturally, whoever does not believe in Jesus, but only sees the general and human in the person of Jesus, and who wishes to see everything that has happened demonstrated by means of the miracle, or whoever believes in Jesus solely on the basis of the miracles—this person will find the miracle a veiling rather than a revelation. What is true about the signs is also true about the words. One man believes and knows, the other neither believes nor knows. One man follows, the other deserts and persecutes him. The world hates Jesus and the disciples love him. Therefore, the appearance of Jesus is the ultimate division that goes to the very depths. A division between light and darkness, the divine and the diabolic, truth and falsehood, life and death.

Indeed, the fourth evangelist is deeply in earnest about the nature of Jesus' life, which is deeply eschatological both in a saving and a judging way. It is the explicit presupposition of the farewell discourses that the unmediated presence, in the person of one become flesh, is broken in the death of Jesus. The experience of the second generation is brought to expression in a passage like that of 16:4ff. when we hear of the death of Jesus as a way to the Father (ὑπάγειν) on the one hand, and also as a separation from the disciples (ἀπέρχεσθαι) who remain on earth without Jesus. As time goes on, what is reported in the tradition about Jesus is more and more seen as belonging to the past. The life of Jesus is not the same for the men of this generation as it was for the disciples who were able to see Jesus, and who were finally given notice by the visible Jesus: "A little while, and you will see me no more" (16:16 and other places). It is also clear that the word of the Risen One to Thomas speaks about those who will come after and who will believe without having seen Jesus (20:29). All of this, of course, points to the readers of the gospel. The stress on the *distance from the life of Jesus* is sharpened considerably by the first section of the gospel, where the disciples are involved in a salvation based on the faith in the *person* of Jesus. Until the hour of his departure, one believed in him as one who could come to Jesus and see him, understand him, and follow him. With the hour of departure, the break with such a faith had to be faced squarely. In that context, the question was whether all faith and all salvation was now in jeopardy because of the departure. The farewell discourses are meant to provoke this question in the reader. The sorrow (λύπη) of the disciples, which filled their hearts at such an announcement (16:6), is at first sight only too consistent in view of the meaning that faith had had until that time.

However, the question is negated, and this is the theological decision of the evangelist: "A little while, and you will see me no more; again a little while, and you will see me" (16:16). This promise points first and foremost to the appearance of the resurrected one.[72] This appearance is not meant in the traditional sense. The traditional Hellenistic concept of Jesus coming out of the realm of death and returning to earth, which is perhaps the motif of the pre-Johannine narration of the appearance of Jesus to Mary Magdalene in John 20:1, 11–18,[73] is denied by the evangelist. He denies this by allowing the resurrected one to say in 20:17: "Do not hold me." A Jesus who returned to earth and who received life back as depicted in the traditional story here does not really exist. Mary is not allowed to "touch" him because he had "not yet ascended to the Father." The meaning of this is that one cannot encounter the risen Jesus as one did the earthly one before his death. Here the point is to have faith without seeing (20:29).

It is important to see that one cannot have Jesus with him again as in the past, but it is just as essential for the post-Easter believer to see that while Jesus of Nazareth has decisively left the earth in the sense of the earthly one born of the flesh, it is nevertheless true that he will return to his own and take them with him (14:2). He is going to the Father, in order that the Father will send the Counselor, the Spirit of Truth. And this sending of the Spirit is an "advantage" to them. The ascent to the Father had the goal of making possible the coming of the Spirit (16:7)! If the whole of Jesus' mission is for the sake of his own, then likewise the ascent in which his mission comes to fulfillment. This fulfillment does not just consist in the reunion of the Ascended One with the Father and his reception into the original glory of the Father (17:5). It is not a matter that affects only himself, but it is also for the good of all who are his. He goes "to prepare a place" (14:2f.), or to incorporate them into his glory, which is to incorporate them into his primal unity with the Father (17:20ff.). The Father and the Son will come and make their abode with the disciples (14:23). This eschatological concept of an eternal union of all the believers with the exalted Jesus, and in him with God himself, is a concept thoroughly gnostic in structure and the fourth evangelist has connected it with the Christian's present possession of the Spirit. The promise of the Comforter (16:5ff.; compare 14:16f.) and the promise of his own return (16:16ff.; compare 14:18ff.) are at times purposely placed in parallel. This means the Spirit, who is experienced in the present, is interpreted as the returning and glorified Jesus.[74] What was true for the earthly Jesus is again valid for the disciples. Wherever they are with the Lord, once with the earthly Jesus, now with the returned and exalted Lord,[75] all divine perfection is present and active. It is the first time that the entire traditional eschatological image is concentrated in the spiritual togetherness with Jesus. This is particularly true of the image of an eschatological and future coming of the exalted Lord from heaven.

It is also in this context that we have the answer of the fourth evangelist to the question of his generation concerning the where of the Christian salvation. While Luke referred to the past of the life of Jesus, and the writer of Hebrews to the imminent eschatological future, the fourth evangelist has worked on the basis of the present experience of the Spirit, which distinguishes, with real finality, the disciples of Jesus from the world that is fundamentally devoid of such experience (14:17). There is a common determining presupposition at the root of every truly Christian solution to the theological problem of the present time. It is one that is common to all three theologians of early Catholicism, and is taken from the oldest tradition of early Christianity, and perhaps—as we see it—taken from Jesus himself. This is that salvation is actualized where the disciple of Jesus is with Jesus. However, each one of them had decided in a specific direction in which the solution was to be found, and this was in light of their own experience of historical time. John solved the question of where the Christian could appropriate his salvation in Jesus by avoiding the past life of Jesus and the eschatological future, and instead concentrating on an experience for the Christian in the present, an experience to make him joyful and certain, because he experienced the essence of things in Jesus himself. This is available to every Christian as a personal experience of the Spirit.

At the same time, his own construction allowed him to answer the additional question concerning the legitimation, the interpretation, and the salvatory meaning of the entire *Jesus tradition*, by which the sphere of tradition in which he had been brought up was determined. The reader of the Gospel of John does not read the book with the eyes of the original disciples, who are described in it, but from the point of view of post-Easter knowledge. Already, the insertion of the well-known liturgical hymn as an introduction made this evident. Also, there are many continually returning individual references that run through the report of the evangelist and can be noticed by the perceptive reader. He reads the presentation of the earthly time of Jesus as an illustration of his present experience, for his own personal experience of the Son of God in the Spirit is presupposed. In view of the essential person of the Son of God in him, the earthly Jesus is one and the same with the exalted Son of God who is experienced in the Spirit. It is also natural for the evangelist to understand that what he had sketched did really happen. From his personal identity, it followed that the whole tradition about the earthly Jesus (throughout all the critical questioning that knew of the historical distance from Jesus that had arisen in the meantime) could be related directly to the post-Easter present. Just as the Christians are themselves clearly involved in the "world" (17:11, 15), so also the exalted Lord, with whom they are united in Spirit, was once "in the flesh." In a similar way, the relationship that the disciples were once reported to have with Jesus is the actual picture of what the Christians can constantly experience in their present time. However, since the earthly event of that time was the decisive sending of the Son by the Father into the midst of the world to be the revelation of God, this past event remains the enduring criterion for every subsequent Christian experience of the Spirit. Seen in this light, the evangelist has done nothing other with his whole work than what he allowed Jesus to describe with respect to the function of the Spirit. The Comforter will "glorify" (16:14) Jesus. He will teach and make them remember all things that the earthly Jesus had once said to them (14:26). In fact, the gospel, as John has conceived it, is a theologically and critically developed example of the activity of the Spirit among the present living Christians.

In this respect, the evangelist gave up the eschatological future in its decisive aspect. In one way, this connects him with Luke, but at the same time there is a great distinction from Luke, who still pays attention to the eschatological tradition in the sense of marking out a future end of time in the history of the church. In contrast, the fourth evangelist has taken away the character of history from the state of participation in salvation (even though outwardly it might look like a part of worldly existence), and in this way he is in opposition to Luke, along with the writer of Hebrews. Both of them are gnostic Christian theologians, but Luke was unacquainted with gnosticism! On the one hand, John could build into his theological scheme the Jesus tradition after having given it such an epiphany-like stamp (a fact he was obliged to do if he did not wish to deprive his congregations of their total stock of tradition); on the other hand, he could not do anything else but eliminate the eschatological elements in the tradition without endangering this tradition in his congregations. He could do so because the Jewish-apocalyptic stamp of this early common eschatology was more or less out of place in the gnostic context.[76] The one expression of a futuristic-eschatological accent still possible in the context of Johannine theology seems to be in I Jn. 3:2: "When he appears we shall be like him, for we shall see him as he is." However, strictly speaking, this passage has already shifted from the ground of the specific theological stand of the fourth evangelist; namely, that the present experience of the Spirit brings the nearness of the Son of God *for* eternity.[77] Thus, in spite of all similarity in the conceptions and terminology, the Gospel of John is to be distinguished from the Johannine epistles.

7. SUMMARY

What has our sketch of the primitive Christian history of tradition to offer in illuminating the systematic issue that we want to serve?

First, the one sure insight: In spite of all the diverse witnesses of primitive Christianity, the common judgment is that revelation, in its fundamentally theological conception, has a very common point in the resurrection of the crucified Jesus from the dead, which is the event by which God ushered in the new age. This is the common fundamental knowledge of the whole of primitive Christianity, and it binds Jew and Gentile together as God's one congregation of salvation. Primitive Christianity has made this knowledge visible and known above all divisions and differences as the historical *Novum*, the new factor within the surrounding world of Judaism and paganism.

In agreement with the Old Testament essay, my introductory section dealing with Judaism has shown that the beginning basic concept of revelation as the self-disclosure of God has in fact arisen out of the genius of the Israelitic understanding of God. Jahweh reveals himself in the context of historical acts. In early Judaism, the self-disclosure of God is awaited as the one encompassing event in the future in which God would bring the whole of human history to its end and goal as a ratification of his primal election in giving eternal salvation to the congregation of the elected righteous, and also the ratification of the sacrilege of all unrighteousness in their eternal negation. This expectation has been the historical presupposition for the primitive Christian faith in Jesus. For its own part, this faith is based on the actuality of the event of Jesus' resurrection as the decisive inauguration of the eschatological self-revelation of God. The early Palestinian congregations acknowledged the resurrection to be God's final confirmation of the unique claims of Jesus about himself. To the extent that Jesus knew and asserted the relation with his person to be decisive in the eschatological salvation or damnation—to this extent it is ultimate after the resurrection to now belong to Jesus in a definitive way in order to be counted among the number of the recipients of salvation who have been saved. The event that has already been inaugurated will catch up the whole cosmos in a universal way. To this extent, the fate of Jesus is understood in connection with the Jewish-apocalyptic thought as the self-revelation of God. Revelation is the one definitive event as the "sum" of universal history.

However, in view of the whole tradition-history of primitive

Christianity, the title *Revelation as History* refers at the same time to a problem that presents itself to theological reflection in an increasingly clear way as one that was there from the outset. According to the apocalyptic view, the future eschatological self-revelation is the conclusion and ratification of all history. Related to the fate of Jesus, this means that the end would now be also there, and correspondingly, primitive Christianity has actually inferred the inauguration of the end out of the event of the resurrection of Jesus as the validity of the earthly Jesus and it has understood the short time between Easter and the factual universal entrance of the *eschaton* as a process of the final events themselves as they develop. Its present appeared to be eschatological time in its own right, *because* Easter was in the past and *therefore* the eternal reunion with the exalted Lord lay ahead.

This total understanding could not present the *past* of the fate of Jesus as a far-removed entity and the *future* of the *eschaton* as the expected and distant future. In the historical accomplishment of the transition from Jewish to Gentile Christianity, this eschatological orientation of the total perspective had visibly altered itself without being widely noticed. The eschatological rejoicing and exuberance in all places obscured the difference in the understanding between the apocalyptically stamped primitive Christian tradition and the Hellenistic and mostly gnostic-thinking Gentile Christianity. Where the apocalyptic thought structure of the history of election was not present, the eschatological Christ event threatened to become an eternal epiphany. In fact, the primitive apocalyptic structure of primitive Christian tradition was essentially altered in this direction, both in the Hellenistic transmission of the traditions about Jesus and in the Hellenistic understanding of the eschatologically stamped mission kerygma. This is shown by the tradition-critical situation of Mark, but even more by the Gospel of John, Hebrews, and the deutero-Pauline epistles. In this literature, the past nature of the Christ event, as well as the eschatological future of the participation in salvation, is referred to the present. How this is done varies. It is accomplished by means of a christological myth or by asserting that the eschatological future is found in Christian existence itself.

In the midst of this fluid transformation, the various debates of Paul with the Judaistic Galatians and the Hellenistic-gnostic Corinthians did serve to clarify for the first time the battle that Paul fought on two fronts. On the one hand, Paul opened the way to the universality of the eschatological event by simultaneously defending the equality of Gentile Christians with regard to the eschatological salvation in Christ, who died for all, while opposing all tendencies to make Christianity into a Jewish sect. On the other hand, he acknowledged the alien influence that gnosticism exercised on the fundamental character of the primitive Christian tradition in its stress on eschatology and election history. Thus, against the tendency of the Corinthians to allow the past event of Christ and the future participation of the Christian's salvation to be contemporized and merge together, Paul for his part stressed the distance between the Christian present and the time of Jesus.

In all likelihood, Paul himself did not realize the full historical implication and importance of his two decisions. Nor could he foresee that Gentile Christianity would very soon become the sole bearer of the Christian tradition, with the inevitable result, namely, the total transition of the Christian tradition into the non-Jewish thought world. Nor could he have known that his stress on the temporal distinction between the Christian and Christ implied a historical distance. By the time of the second generation of Christians, the whole eschatological basis of the primitive Christian tradition was factually out of date by the simple passing of time. It is here that the question first emerges concerning the way in which the *past event of the fate* of Jesus as the eschatological self-revelation is to be related to the continuation of Christian history, and also how the *eschaton* is to be understood as it becomes increasingly separated from the resurrection of Jesus and becomes more of an *isolated event*.

Although there is a considerable reduction from the point of soteriology, Luke has held to the basic point of Paul's decision in this situation by stressing the fate of Jesus as the place of all Christian salvation. It is stressed more in the sense of a past epoch of the "Life of Jesus," and he also assumed a historical mediation of salvation in the course of church history.

In contrast, the Epistle to the Hebrews has made the primitive Christian kerygma of exaltation the base of its theology and has pointed to heaven as the proper place for the realization of salvation and the goal of the pilgrim faith, which can be appropriated most fully only in the time of the eschatological future. Finally, the fourth evangelist radicalized the trend toward contemporaneity in salvation, lifting up the earthly mission of Jesus into an eternally valid image of the present experience of salvation in the Spirit and eliminating the element of futuristic eschatology. How is one to judge these two theological positions that evolved in the gnosticizing situation of second-generation Christianity? Judged by the apocalyptic understanding that founded the primitive Christian faith in the fate of Jesus as an event involving the perfect self-revelation of God, these two theologians appear as threats to the central Christian tradition for depressing the historical aspect of the relationship between the fate of Jesus and salvation. Cut loose from its historical connection with the fate of Jesus, the resurrection of Jesus became an isolated "exaltation" and sooner or later a myth. In the translation of the spiritual experience into terms of contemporaneity with Christ, the past fate of Jesus lost its historical character. This could have resulted in the elimination of the entire Israelite, Jewish, primitive Christian understanding of revelation as the self-revelation of God in history. Neither of these two writers had such a desire, and early Catholicism is thus correct in accepting the Gospel of John and the Epistle to the Hebrews into the canon while condemning the gnostic-Christian positions of the so-called heresies of the second and third centuries.

Still, without the strong influence of the Lucan *heilsgeschichtliche* theology, the church would certainly have run the danger of losing the heritage of the apocalyptic structure of concepts, and with this it would also have lost the knowledge of the historically occurring self-revelation of God as the salvation of all men, a fact that is fundamental for the Christian faith. In spite of all the justifiable criticism of this evangelist, the church can truly thank Luke for his decisive role in the protection of the historical aspect of primitive Christian tradition in the Hellenistic world.

NOTES

1. *Der Begriff der Offenbarung im Neuen Testament*, Munich, 1949. Miss Schulte has seen the necessity of probing the important exegetical question of the relation between the modern theological conceptualization of revelation and the corresponding terms in the New Testament.
2. See above, p. 3.
3. The essay of Rudolf Bultmann, "The Concept of Revelation in the New Testament," in *Existence and Faith*, pp. 58–91, is an example of how a study of revelation in primitive Christianity almost amounts to a basic blueprint for a "Theology of the New Testament." With a total neglect of the terminological data, Bultmann developed a statement of the preunderstanding of revelation, in order to delineate from this perspective an understanding of the Christ event and its significance as the answer to the question of human existence according to revelation. The essay you are now reading ought to be distinguished from that of Bultmann's by its different preunderstanding of revelation. While Bultmann allowed the structure of revelation to be defined by an anthropological presupposition and consequently starts a very general concept of revelation, our investigation will proceed from a strongly theological concept of revelation as the self-disclosure of God, as used in the structure and intention of Jewish and primitive Christian theology. This is also the more or less common legacy of the most recent history of theology. From this it follows that the over-all plan of a New Testament theology which Bultmann first laid down in 1929 can no longer be taken over. Rather, the structure of a theology of the New Testament must be thought through anew from the ground up.
4. See pp. 25–48.
5. See p. 33.
6. See v. Rad, *TWNT*, II, p. 244. The point to note is the close connection between

this concept of the impending appearance of the glory of Jahweh and the traditional formula of the knowledge of God on the basis of his acts; see pp. 101f.

7. Schemone Esra, Benediction 1.

8. *Ibid.*, Benediction 2.

9. *Ibid.*, Benedictions 10 and 11, in which it says: "Bring again our judges as before, and our counsellors as at the beginning, and you alone be king over us."

10. *Ibid.*, Benediction 14.

11. See A. Oepke, *TWNT*, III, p. 577.

12. See Karl Georg Kuhn, *TWNT*, I, pp. 571f., with the proof given from Strack-Billerbeck, I, p. 179.

13. On this see Dietrich Rössler, *Gesetz und Geschichte*, Neukirchen, 1960, pp. 20ff., esp. p. 33.

14. The term "revelation" is the usual expression in the apocalyptic texts for the eschatological participation in the gifts of salvation that the elect have from God when they enter the new aeon.

15. See *CD B* 20:25f. and 1*QM* 11:8; 12:7, 12; 13:7ff.

16. See Rössler, *op. cit.*, p. 98.

17. See pp. 86f.

18. *TWNT*, III, p. 581.

19. See Rössler, *op. cit.*, pp. 56ff.

20. This can be shown even by the terminology, in that such visions can be designated "revelation" with the same term that also means the end of history itself.

21. While this or that individual passage might carry with it a very powerful "feeling of anticipation" for the contingent eschatological future (as for instance the description of the end in Dan. 12:6f., etc.) this ought not to be thought of as the unique characteristic of apocalyptic literature. It is not a question of making "calculations," but of correcting the received proleptic revelation with a view to history in its present reality. *God* alone is the one who leads up to the end, and he *will truly* do just that. This is the perspective of such statements, which can be relatively easily altered or neglected in the apocalyptic traditions when it is clear that they are in error. See such a process in Dan. 12:11f.

22. The frequent address "Rabbi" is due to lack of any other term that could be applied to the appearance and life of this wandering preacher and his relationship with disciples. This is also found in apocalyptic traditions. Enoch, for example, who is really the recipient of apocalyptic revelation, is also addressed as Rabbi (Eth. Enoch 15:1; cf. 12:3f. and 92:1).

23. See W. G. Kümmel, "Jesus und die jüdische Traditionsgedanke," *ZNW*, 33, 1934, p. 125. Previous to this, G. Dalman, *Jesus-Jeschua* (Macmillan), pp. 69f., and Strack-Billerbeck, I, pp. 253f.

24. ἔνοχος ἔσται τῇ κρίσει is meant in verse 22a in an eschatological way, and its relationship to the earthly juridical situation (see v. 22b) is secondary. In this case, Bultmann's observation is correct. Bultmann, *The History of the Synoptic Tradition* (Harper & Row, 1962), p. 134.

25. See W. Bacher, *Die exegetische Terminologie der jüdischen Traditionsliteratur*, II, 1905, p. 189. Further, esp. J. Abrahams, *Studies in the Pharisäism and the Gospels*,

I, 1917, p. 16. More recently, G. Barth, G. Bornkamm, and H. J. Held, *Tradition and Interpretation in Matthew* (SCM), pp. 93ff.

26. See the material in W. Bacher, *Tradition und Tradenten in den Schulen Palästinas und Babyloniens*, 1914, pp. 156ff.

27. ἐρρέθη is a paraphrastic way of indicating the divine origin of the prohibition. See A. Schlatter, *Der Evangelist Matthäus*, 4th ed., 1957, p. 165.

28. A discussion of the striking self-consciousness of the so-called "teacher of righteousness" in the Qumran literature might be of help, but I have set it aside here due to the lack of any definitive conclusions as far as this subject is concerned.

29. "The Problem of the Historical Jesus," in *Essays on New Testament Themes* (SCM Studies in Biblical Theology, no. 41), pp. 15ff.

30. See for example the introduction to the speech on idols in Eth. Enoch 37:4: "Till the present day such wisdom has never been given by the Lord of Spirits as I have received according to my insight, according to the good pleasure of the Lord of Spirits by whom the lot of eternal life has been given to me." Cited from R. H. Charles, *The Apocrypha and Pseudepigrapha of the Old Testament*, vol. II (Oxford), p. 209.

31. This does not mean that the special claim of Jesus comes directly out of apocalyptic tradition.

32. See K. G. Kuhn, *TWNT*, I, pp. 570ff.

33. See the Aramaic text in P. Fiebig, *Jesus Bergpredigt*, 1924, p. 50, and the German translation on pp. 106f. On the question of introductions, see I. Elbogen, *Der jüdische Gottesdienst in seiner geschichtlichen Entwicklung*, 3rd ed., 1931, pp. 92ff.: "May his great name be made great and holy in the world which he created according to his will. May he let his kingdom rule in your life now and in the time to come." See also the eschatological petition in Schemone Esra's Benediction 11. See note 9.

34. See J. Jeremias, "Kennzeichen der ippissima vox Jesu," *Festschrift A. Wikenhauser, Synoptische Studien*, 1954, pp. 88f. These observations go back to G. Dalman, *The Word of Jesus* (T & T. Clark), pp. 190f. See also G. Kittel, *TWNT*, I, pp. 5ff.

35. See, for example, the series of sayings on anxiety in Q, Mt. 6:25ff., Lk. 12:22ff., where the everyday care of God for the birds of the heaven, the lilies of the field, and the anxiety of man is linked directly with the Kingdom of God, which is at hand. Thus, the admonition is: "But seek first his Kingdom and his righteousness, and all these things shall be yours as well." In the perspective of Jesus, to surrender to God the cares of everyday and to be oriented to an attentive expectation of the impending reign of God is the same thing. There is a widely held notion that the stress on the nearness of the Kingdom of God has no relation to the motif-complex of "creation," "providence," and "everyday life" (see esp. H. Conzelmann, "Zur Methode der Leben-Jesu-Forschung" *ZThK*, 56, 1959, Beiheft 1, pp. 10ff., and the article "Jesus Christ," in *RGG.*, 3rd ed., pp. 633f.). This is a misconception because the immediacy in which both concepts stand to God is grounded in the eschatological understanding of Jesus and summed up in the formula ἤγγικεν ἡ βασιλεία τῶν οὐρανῶν.

36. On the following see H. E. Tödt, *The Son of Man in the Synoptic Tradition* (Westminster), pp. 31ff.

37. H. Conzelmann, *RGG*, III, col. 641ff., rightly emphasizes this. When, however,

on p. 645 he refuses to see in Lk. 12:8 a saying of Jesus, because he sees no
room in Jesus' eschatology "for an eschatological perfector figure except for
Jesus himself," he overlooks that in this saying Jesus is merely representative
of the eschatological judgment. The saying intends to relate the present
relationship with Jesus to the judgment of the Son of Man. See also Tödt, *op.
cit.*, pp. 339ff.

38. Note early form of the end of the beatitudes in Mt. 5:11, which is ἕνεκεν ἐμοῦ,
and how this becomes developed in Lk. 6:22 to ἕνεκεν τοῦ υἱοῦ τοῦ ἀνθρώπου.
On the other hand, note how the more primitive "Son of man" in the Q-saying
of Lk. 12:8 develops into the "I" of Mt. 10:32.

39. A review of the apocalyptic understanding of the Torah will show it to be the
presupposition for the antipharisaic interpretation of the Law in the teaching
of Jesus. The function of Jesus in his person is to become the place of the
eschatological salvation for his disciples. The confession of Jesus and the
verification of this in discipleship of him make manifest the existing eschatological designation of the disciple. In the apocalyptic understanding, the
Torah had a similar function. Disregard the eschatology of Jesus for a moment.
Whoever keeps the Law is just. The just also belong to the elect, who will be
made into recipients of salvation on the last day. Now, Jesus, in his own
person, has taken over this function for his disciples. Because of the nearness
of the rule of God, there is a *direct* correspondence between the place of
salvation and the place of the discipleship of Jesus. We must now try to
understand the Rabbinic-pharisaic understanding and interpretation of the
Law with the help of the apocalyptic preunderstanding. Then we must step
from the general apocalyptic eschatology to the specific eschatology of Jesus,
and then we will see the necessity of Jesus' sharply antipharisaic polemic.

40. On this see G. Ebeling, "Jesus and the Faith," in *Word and Faith* (Fortress),
pp. 201ff., who has caught on to something very important with regard to the
proclamation of Jesus, although he is a bit too dependent on the synoptic
πίστις material and its relation to Jesus.

41. See the Old Testament essay on pp. 29ff. and 39.

42. See especially Is. 35:5f., as well as the material in P. Volz, *Die Eschatologie der
jüdischen Gemeinde*, 2nd ed., 1934, pp. 381ff.

43. See Tödt, *op. cit.*, pp. 224ff.

44. On this see W. Kümmel, "Kirchenbegriff und Geschichtsbewusstsein in der
Urgemeinde und bei Jesus," in *Symbolae biblicae Uppsalienses*, I, 1943, pp. 13.

45. See my article "Das religionsgeschichtliche Problem der Bekehrung des
Paulus," *ΖThK*, 56, 1959, pp. 273ff.

46. Compare the passages I Thess. 1:9f. with 4:13f., the schema of the sermons
that underlie the preaching of Paul in the Lucan Acts (14:15ff. and 17:22ff.),
and finally the constitutive element in the catechetical material of Heb. 6:2.
On the analysis of the particulars of these texts, see my book *Die Missionsreden
der Apostelgeschichte*, 1961, pp. 8off.

47. See, for example, Gal. 3:2f. The beginning occurred in the Spirit, which the
converts had received in connection with their baptism.

48. There are individual passages like Gal. 5:22 where Paul counts faith as one
of the fruits of the Spirit, or I Cor. 12:9, which speaks of πίστις ἐν τῷ αὐτῷ
πνεύματι, or II Cor. 4:13 with the formula τὸ πνεῦμα τῆς πίστεως. These are
understood falsely if they are taken as important theologoumena about the
pneumatic establishment of faith.

49. The passage in II Cor. 3:17f., which has often been wrongly interpreted, does not deal with Jesus, but with God as the one who was the κύριος in the Old Testament citation in v. 16, and who is understood as πνεῦμα by Paul in v. 17. It is through this that the Christian experiences the changing likeness of "the glory of God in the face of Christ" (4:6).

50. See R. Bultmann, *Glauben und Verstehen*, I, 2nd ed., 1954, pp. 40ff.; W. Schmithals, *Die Gnosis in Korinth*, 1956; and my book *Weisheit und Torheit*, esp. pp. 205ff.

51. In the expression of the death ὑπὲρ ἡμῶν, Paul took over an expression from the tradition, which he had already found in connection with the previously established mission kerygma. (See esp. I Cor. 15:3f.) However, in Paul's theology this was placed in the center of his Christ kerygma, a place it would not have in the previous tradition.

52. This bracketing of the past, present, and the future in the differentiation between the fate of Jesus and the participation in it (which continues in Christian existence until the coming of the end) was a development that had an essential meaning for Paul's theology ever since he had his great confrontation with the Corinthian congregation. (See esp. Rom. 5–6, and 8:17ff.) However, the complex of concepts was not in itself an original work of Paul. It was already available to him in the tradition, though in a much simpler form. This can be seen in the writer of I Peter, who, largely out of a lack of any ambition to theological originality, simply passed on in a rather unreflective way the Hellenistic Christian tradition of the environment as influenced by Paul. The concepts that appear in the proem betray a horizon of apocalyptic theology, with all its details. "Through the resurrection of Jesus Christ from the dead," and by God's mercy, the Christians were "born anew" to the hope of the reception of life in the coming eschaton (1:3). Therefore, their hope lay ready for them in heaven (v. 7), and God himself guards them in the present until they receive the inheritance (v. 5), and so they rejoice even now (v. 6ff.) in eschatological joy, for although they are persecuted and afflicted in many ways, their coming salvation is secure through their trust in the coming Jesus. On the basis of a proleptic revelation (v. 12), the prophets of the Old Testament predicted by the "Spirit of Christ" (v. 11) the sufferings of Jesus and his subsequent glory. What was prophesied is now fulfilled. Not only was the fate of Christ proclaimed to the Christians as their immediate salvation (v. 12), but also they themselves have participation in the sufferings of Christ, in their own afflictions that are currently oppressing them. Since the glorification of Christ followed on his suffering, they too have a participation in his glory when this "is to be revealed" in the final event (4:13, 5:1). The fate of Christ is here understood apocalyptically as a preview of the end. His "suffering" is the sum total of the frightful afflictions and catastrophes that are expected at the end of this age and that will overtake the elect. (See D. Rössler, *op. cit.*, pp. 88f.) Likewise, his subsequent glorification (1:11) is participation in the salvation prepared beforehand. This development of the eschatological fate of Christ is also marked out for the post-Easter history of the Christian community. Presently, they are enduring the oppressions of the end as a saving participation in the suffering of Christ, because in this way they have a share in the fate of Christ that is now being perfected. This means that their future is also secure as participation in the glorification of Christ. This complex of concepts is received from Paul (see esp. Rom. 8:17), and the Hellenistic baptismal

tradition is changed through his influence. In the Hellenistic version, the baptized become one with the death *and* resurrection of Christ. (See esp. Col. 2:12 and 3:1–4.) In contrast to this, Paul understood baptism as participation in the death of Christ, while he waited for the participation in the eschatological-proleptic fate of Christ, and this is in closer correspondence to the understanding of "suffering" in the tradition of I Peter, because the participation in the resurrection of Christ is awaited in the imminent future (Rom. 6:5, 8).

53. See W. Schmithals, *op. cit.*, pp. 134ff., and my book *Weisheit und Torheit*, pp. 11ff.; and for another point of view, D. Georgi, *Die Gegner des Paulus im 2. Korintherbrief* (Diss. Heidelberg), 1958.

54. See on this the essay of mine mentioned in note 45.

55. The Pauline texts contain no evidence that Paul used the synoptic material about Jesus, or even that he presupposed this in his congregations. Everything seems to speak against the widely held hypothesis (especially among Catholics) that, while the letters of Paul did not bring this out, it is true that he made extensive use of the material about the life of Jesus in his mission sermons. However, on the other side of the coin, it is debatable how one could explain the absence of synoptic material in Paul. There is certainly insufficient evidence that Paul had consciously excluded this material from his proclamation. The theological intent that must then be imputed to Paul will simply not hold up in the Pauline conception of theology, for it would be a totally gnostic intent. (On the text II Cor. 5:16, see the evaluation of this as a "secondary, Corinthian, gnostic gloss," in W. Schmithals, "Zwei gnostische Glossen im 2. Korintherbrief," *Ev. Theol.*, 18, 1958, pp. 552ff.) But then it is to be assumed that even the Syrian mission tradition out of which Paul came did not have the synoptic material about Jesus—no matter how difficult this historical explanation might seem to be.

56. See W. Marxsen, *Der Evangelist Markus*, 2nd ed., 1959, pp. 77f.

57. See E. Grässer, *Der Problem der Parusieverzögerung in den synoptischen Evangelien und in der Apostelgeschichte*, 1957.

58. See especially H. Conzelmann, *The Theology of St. Luke* (Harper & Row), 1960.

59. On this see the analysis in my book *Die Missionsreden der Apostelgeschichte*.

60. See on this Acts 5:32, and the remarkably parallel positioning of the witness of the apostles and the bestowal of the Spirit on them.

61. This was first seen by H. Conzelmann, *The Theology of St. Luke*; see esp. pp. 131ff.

62. See E. Lohse, "Lukas als Theologe der Heilsgeschichte," *Ev. Theol.*, 14, 1954, pp. 256ff.

63. The theological criticism of the Lucan position, which cannot be developed here, ought to stress two items: First, the correct starting point of his solution within the given factors in his historical situation; and secondly, the essential shortcomings and danger in the position that he did work out. On this see my book *Die Missionsreden der Apostelgeschichte*, pp. 193ff.

64. See esp. G. Bornkamm, "Das Bekenntnis im Hebräerbrief," in *Studien zu Antike und Urchristentum*, 1959, pp. 188ff.

65. The detailed anti-Jewish and polemic discussion in the middle section of the epistle, chapters 7–10, recapitulates this central thesis.

66. On this conception see especially M. Dibelius, "Der himmlische Kultus nach dem Hebräerbrief," in *Botschaft und Geschichte*, II, 1956, pp. 160ff.

67. *Das wandernde Gottesvolk*, 2nd ed., 1957.
68. That the gospel of John originates in oriental gnostic Christianity is a rather widely held view in present-day research. See esp. R. Bultmann, *Theology of the New Testament*, vol. II, pp. 15ff., also *RGG*, 3rd ed., III, col. 849; E. Schweitzer, *EGO EIMI*, 1939; E. Haenchen, "Johanneische Probleme," in *ZThK*, 56, 1959, p. 53; see also S. Schulz, *Untersuchungen zur Menschensohn-christologie im Johannesevangelium*, 1957, pp. 175.; and also now *Komposition und Herkunft der johanneischen Reden*, 1960, pp. 182ff.
69. E. Käsemann has rightly shown this in his analysis of the prologue; see "Aufbau und Anliegen des Johanneischen Prologs," in *Libertas Christiana, Festschrift F. Delekat*, 1957, pp. 75ff., and esp. pp. 90ff.
70. It is the intention of the introductory pericope (1:35f.) to lay out this structure of faith in a programmatic way. After the person to the person of Jesus, his disciples follow Jesus to see "where he [Jesus] was staying," and they were obliged to "come and see," and they "stayed" with him (1:39), so that their faith was mediated to others in the surrounding country who also came, saw, and stayed. "Come and see," is what Philip said to Nathaniel (1:46), and this is what Jesus had previously said to the two disciples (1:39). Also, the Samaritans who were brought out by the woman said: "It is no longer because of your words that we believe, for we have heard for ourselves [namely, in confrontation with the *person* of Jesus], and we know that this is indeed the Saviour of the world" (4:42).
71. Compare especially the prayer of Jesus in 11:42, which interprets the miracle in this sense.
72. This promise does not concern an eschatological return of Jesus as in the "second coming" in the Epistle to the Hebrews (see p. 100 on Heb. 9:28).
73. See R. Bultmann, *Das Evangelium des Johannes*, 1950, pp. 528f. A. Kragerud, *Der Lieblingsjünger im Johannesevangelium*, 1959, pp. 29f., guesses that a traditional story about Peter forms the background, while the evangelist has inserted here the Beloved Disciple.
74. There is in the tradition of the evangelist the demonstration of the pierced side and the nailed hands of Jesus (in contrast to the forceful command of Jesus that Mary is not to touch him—20:17). The evangelist took over this tradition for the purpose of stressing the identity of the exalted Lord, returning in the Spirit, with the earthly Jesus. In 20:29 it is unambiguously clear that while the demands of Thomas (20:25) were acceded to on one occasion, they are not really appropriate to the new situation where the exalted Lord returns in the Spirit to the post-Easter Christian.
75. 14:13; 17:24 (see 10:29); 12:26; see, in view of the Spirit, 14:16.
76. Throughout the Johannine material there are interpolations in the text by a radical like 5:28f. (an apparent correction of 5:24f.); 6:39f., 44, and 54. These interpretations show that the critical Johannine solution gave offense in such a sphere of tradition.
77. Note the εἰς τὸν αἰῶνα in 14:16.

IV

Dogmatic Theses on the Doctrine of Revelation

Wolfhart Pannenberg

THESIS 1: THE SELF-REVELATION OF GOD IN THE BIBLICAL WITNESSES IS NOT OF A DIRECT TYPE IN THE SENSE OF A THEOPHANY, BUT IS INDIRECT AND BROUGHT ABOUT BY MEANS OF THE HISTORICAL ACTS OF GOD

In developing this thesis, I wish to draw together the results of the exegetical investigations and expand them with particular reference to the question of the indirectness (or directness) of revelation.

The Old Testament essay has shown that a decisive insight concerning revelation is found in the Israelite traditions, in which an understanding of Jahweh is obtained through his historical activity. The earlier traditions about appearances of Jahweh which were connected closely with Israel's cult and place of worship are suppressed and displaced by the thought that Jahweh is to be revealed in his acts in history. At first, this idea was linked most vividly with the exodus from Egypt, which ancient Israel took as Jahweh's primal act of salvation. Statements to this effect can already be found in the Jahwistic tradition, which makes no significant distinction between the miracles of Moses in Egypt and Jahweh's own decisive act of judgment at the Reed Sea. Both are proofs of the deity and power of Jahweh. The writer sees the purpose of the Egyptian plagues in terms of their effect in causing Pharaoh to acknowledge the power of Jahweh and thus bring about the release of the Israelites (Ex. 7:17; 8:16, 18; 9:14). At the end of the narration relating the escape through the Reed Sea and the destruction of the Egyptians, the Jahwist says: "And Israel saw the great work which the Lord did against the Egyptians, and the people feared the Lord; and they believed in the Lord and his servant Moses" (Ex. 14:31). According to this, faithful trust was effected by the evidence of historical facts that brought about salvation and revealed Jahweh's deity and power.

In Deuteronomy, the attention is not on the single events, but on the complex of exodus and occupancy of the land, all of which is viewed as the self-vindication of Jahweh: "And because he loved your fathers and chose their descendants after them, and brought you out of Egypt with his own presence, by his great power, driving out before you nations greater and mightier than yourselves, to bring you in, to give you their land for an inheritance, as at this day: know therefore this day, and lay it to your heart, that the Lord is God in heaven above and on the earth beneath; there is no other. Therefore, you shall keep his statutes and his commandments, which I command you this day" (Dt. 4:37-40; compare 7:7-11). The last sentence shows that the authority of God's judgment is grounded in the historical self-vindication of Jahweh for rescuing Israel from Egypt and for giving the land. This does not mean that through this act Jahweh has proved that he is God in a manner analogous to the confrontation with Pharaoh. In this action of rescuing and giving he has proved himself to be *their* God, for he has acted on *their* behalf. The exodus and the occupancy of the land are established as the decisive factor in the knowledge of God, and this is so stated in Hosea and later in Jeremiah.[1]

The prophets, however, especially those of the time of the exile, no longer took the events connected with the occupancy of the land as the ultimate self-vindication of Jahweh. In Isaiah it is clear that the election of Zion and the House of David were added to the above in the tradition of Judah. Isaiah proclaims the fall of the nation and the new activity of salvation anticipated in this as the new self-vindication of Jahweh through which his deity will be demonstrated before the eyes of the nations. Next to Ezekiel, it is second Isaiah who has, more than anyone, proclaimed the proof of the deity of Jahweh as the aim of the newly introduced and still-imminent activity of salvation.[2] As was shown in the New Testament essay, the apocalyptic literature advanced this aspect of the Old Testament's understanding of revelation. The apocalyptic writings expect the final and ultimate self-vindication of Jahweh in connection with the end event, and envision his appearance in glory. This expectation is also part of the apocalyptic horizon in the proclamation of Jesus. But his appearance compressed the content so that the sharp distinction between the times vanishes, and from this springs the framework of apocalyptic theology. This is particularly evident in the first petition of the Lord's Prayer: "May your name be kept holy." It is only within this tradition of prophetic and apocalyptic expectation that it is possible to understand the resurrection of Jesus and his pre-Easter life as a reflection of the eschatological self-vindication of Jahweh.

An investigation of the New Testament's concept of the self-revelation of God in the fate of Jesus does not depend solely on terms that are used for revelation. If one proceeds from ἀπο-καλύπτειν and φανεροῦν alone, as H. Schulte has done, then one finds no statement at all about God's self-revelation. An investigation of the christological titles does not carry us much further. On the other hand, the conception of the *glory of God* often designates with precision his becoming manifest. This is true in the New Testament as well as in the apocalyptic literature.

It is well known that the background of this New Testament concept is many-sided.[3] The idea goes back to both Old Testament and gnostic roots. As von Rad has demonstrated, the כבד יהוה in the Old Testament is already connected with Jahweh's becoming manifest.[4] Isaiah, for instance, saw such manifestations in all earthly events (Is. 6). The manifestation of the glory of Jahweh is generally bound up with his acts, especially those historical acts connected with the emergence of

Israel. The priestly document is acquainted with an appearance of the glory in the exodus history and in the institution of the cult. Since the time of the postexilic prophets, the appearance (or the reappearance) of the glory has become a future event (see Is. 43:1ff.), and an "established element of the eschatological hope" (v. Rad). We note especially the expression of second Isaiah that speaks of the revelatory meaning of the future unveiling of glory. The goal of second Isaiah's vision about a highway in the wilderness, over which God will bring back the exiles, is seen in Is. 40:5: "And the glory of the Lord shall be revealed, and all flesh[!] shall see it together" (see 66:18f.). The priestly document expressly links the concept of glory with the formula of acknowledgment: "And the Egyptians shall know that I am the Lord, when I have gotten glory over Pharaoh, his chariots, and his horsemen" (Ex. 14:18). This is the priestly recension of the passage through the Reed Sea. Although formulated only in words, the glorification of Jahweh through his acts in history is clearly an expression pointing to the indirect revelation of his deity in those acts (see also Ex. 16:6). In this respect, it becomes clear just how far the apocalyptic hope in the future manifestation of present realities in salvation and judgment is also a matter of God revealing himself. Thus, in the apocalyptic theology, the revelation of the glory of God persists until the final event and in this the salvation of the elect is revealed.[5]

However, it is not only in the texts of the Old Testament and in the apocalyptic literature that the concept of glory plays an essential role.[6] This is also true for the gnostic texts. In the Magic Papyri from Egypt, the sorcerer prays to Isis: "Glorify me as I have glorified the name of your son Horos"—a formula very reminiscent of John 17. Naturally, in this text the historical event is not the means of the many-sided glorification and, particularly, it is not expected as a cosmic end event.

In comparison to the gnostic doxa-thought, the Pauline usage is closer to the Old Testament and apocalyptic conception of the glory of God. The glory of God is visible to Paul in the fate of Jesus, whom he emphatically proclaimed as the Crucified One (II Cor. 4:6). God is indirectly revealed in the fate of Jesus. The apocalyptic revelation of his glory in the end judgment has come to pass ahead of time in this fate. In Paul and other New Testament writings, the concept of δόξα has its place in the terminological complex of ἀποκάλυψις in much the same way as in the apocalyptic literature.[7] The revelation of God's glory is also part of the established content of the primitive Christian and apocalyptic expectation. Because the imminent *eschaton* has broken in with the fate of Jesus, the glory of God is already present in the proclamation of the gospel (II Cor. 3). Thus, the congregations united with Christ and living in the hope of their own resurrection already have the πνεῦμα τῆς δόξης (I Pet. 4:14), the "eschatological gift of the Spirit."[8] Because the Spirit is the specific form of reality in the new aeon, the event of Christ is itself spiritual as the eschatological event, and the resulting participation in the Spirit mediated through the proclamation of this event and faith in it (Gal. 3:2 and 14) is the earnest money on the future glory (I Cor. 1:22, 5:2; Rom. 8:23). In this sense Paul can give relatively free reign to the gnostic concept of the Spirit and even say that the Spirit searches the depths of the deity (I Cor. 2:10). But we should not forget that for Paul himself such expressions are always related to the horizon of the eschatological future. And since the past event of salvation, the future of the faithful, and the present of the Spirit are all bound together in the eschatological nearness of God, the apportionment of weight to these three elements is no problem for him. As Wilkens has shown, this was altered in the case of the primitive Christian witnesses of the second generation. They were the first to see the distinction between the present moment and the fate of Jesus as a problem. For them, the center of gravity in the revelation of God could only be in the past, or in the present, or in the future. For Luke, it is in the past. The eschatological future recedes into the undefined distance. It is worth noting that, along with the recession of the eschatological horizon, Luke does not explicitly characterize the event of salvation as revelation. In John the accent is on the present experience of the Spirit. In this case, there are also gnostic lines of thought that come to the fore in the conception of revelation. There is a directness in the gnostic thinking about revelation that is in the tradition that John draws on and that is expressed in the epiphany-like nature of the Christ figure. This directness is broken in John by his reshaping of the Christ event with a stress on its past character. Thus, the Christians of the second generation perceived the glory of God in Christ only indirectly. The experience of the Spirit in the Gospel of John is linked to the Christ of the past, who is consciously thought of as a figure in the past (John 16:14; cf. 14:26). It is only with such a presupposition that one can come to anything like an understandable conception of John's gospel. It is of course true that his presentation of the activity of Jesus himself is still largely styled like a direct manifestation.

What is true for John holds also for Hebrews in many respects. Also, with Hebrews the relation to the past event of Jesus is unbalanced. On the one hand, it is the point of departure for faith, and on the other hand, it is contemporized by a gnostic stylization (Heb. 2:14f.). However, the accent is different, for Hebrews points to the future of salvation. Thus John as well as Hebrews held fast to the past event of Jesus as the norm for the Christian participation in salvation, in spite of their gnostic characteristics. Hebrews stresses the future, and Luke, for his part, emphasizes the present participation of salvation in the Spirit. However, the stress on the past life of Jesus, which is not brought to a close, is carried out with more decisiveness by Luke than by the other two theologians. In this respect, they maintained a peculiar balance between present and past and thus brought the soteriological character of the Christ event to expression in a convincing way.

In this situation, the dogmatic conception of revelation must first of all orient itself to the chain of tradition, which runs from the Old Testament through the apocalyptic literature and on to the proclamation of Jesus found in the first community and in Paul. It must do this so that the specific theological motifs that lay at the base of the New Testament witnesses of the second generation will be kept in view. For one thing, the past character of the event of Jesus ought not be dissolved into a mere "that," but should also have the substance of a "what."

Also, the eschatological qualification of the present, by means of the Christ event and the future salvation, is not lost.

THESIS 2: REVELATION IS NOT COMPREHENDED COMPLETELY IN THE BEGINNING, BUT AT THE END OF THE REVEALING HISTORY

The linking of revelation with the end of history is related to its indirect character. It follows directly out of the indirectness of the divine self-vindication, and without this presupposition revelation cannot be understood.

We have seen that the revelation of God is the defined goal of the present events of history. And only after their occurrence is God's deity perceived. Thus, placing revelation at the close of history is grounded in the indirectness of revelation.

This proves to be valuable knowledge if one is not involved with single revelatory events, but with a series of occurrences. We have already seen that the Old Testament's understanding of revelation tended in this direction. In the development from the Jahwistic tradition to the apocalyptic literature, it is not just the extent of events proving the deity of God that is increasing, but also the content of revelation that is continually revising itself. What had previously been the final vindication of God is now seen as only one step in the ever-increasing context of revelation.

At first, individual events were credited with revealing Jahweh's deity, as, for instance, in the Jahwistic tradition. But in the later words of the prophets, a much more comprehensive plan of Jahweh's history is usually presupposed. Since the time of the Deuteronomist, the total activity, which has a relatively extensive horizon, becomes the means for the self-vindication of Jahweh. We saw that Dt. 4:37ff. understood the deity of God as the result of a whole complex of history, a historical complex that extended from the promises to the fathers to the fulfilling of these in the occupancy of the land. It is not just through the single events of this long history, but rather at the end, in the fulfillment of the promises to the fathers, that Jahweh's deity is proved. For the Deuteronomist, the occupancy of the land was the close of revelatory history. After that event, one can look back to the revelation of Jahweh as one would on a closed event.

All of this was altered with the fall of Judah and the exile from the promised land. The prophets of the exile looked forward to the decisive event of salvation, which now, for the first time, was in the future. The decisive and ultimate revelation of Jahweh was also removed to the future.

In apocalyptic thought, the spiritual situation is substantially sharpened. Not only is the decisive event of salvation always in the future, but the meaning of the present event is, in general, totally hidden. Thus, the continuity from the present to the future is not easily discerned. The two aeons stand in juxtaposition. For apocalyptic thought, the present is filled with tribulation. It is only in the time of the eschatological inauguration of the new aeon that the meaning of the present time is revealed. The destiny of mankind, from creation onward, is seen to be the unfolding according to a plan of God. The apocalyptic thought conceives of a universal history. Thus, the revelation of God and his glory is transferred to the end of all events. That the end will make manifest the secrets of the present is also the presupposition of primitive Christianity.

The history that demonstrates the deity of God is broadened to include the totality of all events. This corresponds completely to the universality of Israel's God, who is not only the God of Israel, but will be the God of all men. This broadening of the *Heilsgeschichte* to a universal history is in essence already accomplished in the major prophets of Israel in that they treat the kingdoms of the world as responsible to God's commands.[9] With the exception of the lists in Chronicles, this point of view is first carried through systematically in apocalyptic literature. Since the time of the Deuteronomist and the prophets of the exile, the God of Israel was known as the Lord of all. Correspondingly, the apocalyptic viewpoint conceived of Jahweh's Law as the ground of the totality of world events. It is at the end of this chain of world events that God can for the first time be revealed with finality as the one true God.

This concept of history determined the Western philosophy of history up to the time of Hegel and Marx. Both conceived of history with a view to its end. For Marx, the revolution of the proletariat will bring an end to all previous history and reveal the humanity of man. Of course Hegel firmly maintains that the Christ event is the one revelation of God; but insofar as he understood his own time and his own philosophy as the kairos for the universal comprehension of history, he also brings it into concurrence with the revelation of Christ.

Placing the manifestation of God at the end of history means that the biblical God has, so to speak, his own history. That is, the historical event of revelation cannot be thought of in an outward way as revealing the essence of God. It is not so much the course of history as it is the end of history that is at one with the essence of God. But insofar as the end presupposes the course of history, because it is the perfection of it, then also the course of history belongs in essence to the revelation of God, for history receives its unity from its goal. Although the essence of God is

from everlasting to everlasting the same, it does have a history
in time. Thus it is that Jahweh first becomes the God of all
mankind in the course of the history that he has brought to be.

This is a history-of-religion statement, and it produces many
consequences for the relation of theology to the science of
religion. The beginnings of Israel develop only gradually out
of the religious environment of the ancient Orient and in this
way it has a distinct antecedent: even in its later stages Israel
retains connections with this heritage. Israel is not to be
artificially isolated from its environment by the assertion of a
supernatural revelation that took place at the time of its
beginnings. Such an assertion would be arbitrarily limited to
the "sacred" region of a *Heilsgeschichte* (in its most disreputable
sense). Such an assertion is unnecessary and meaningless if we
understand that revelation does not have its place in the
beginning, but at the end of history. The earliest appearances
of Jahweh are to be understood as the appearance of a numinous
being, not just from the phenomenological point of view, but
theologically as well. This being may be a numinous being of a
special type, but it is a special type known within the history
of religion. It is only in the course of this history brought about
by Jahweh that this tribal God proves himself to be the one
true God. This proof will be made in the strict and ultimate
sense only at the end of all history. However, in the fate of
Jesus, the end of history is experienced in advance as an anticipation. As we now conceptualize more precisely—it is only in
view of the end that we can say God has proved himself in the
fate of Jesus as the one true God. It is not by chance that the
salvation now is for the Gentile also. This is a necessity because
in the fate of Jesus as the anticipation of the end of all history,
God is revealed as the one God of all mankind who had been
expected since the times of the prophets. The inclusion of the
heathen belonged to the universality of the eschatological
revelation of God. Thus, it is appropriate that the proclamation
of the God who raised Jesus would be tested by means of Greek

philosophy and its questions about God, for philosophy is that discipline that raises the question of the true form of God for all men. Where the eschatological self-revelation of the God of Israel was proclaimed as the one God of all men, this question could not be overlooked, although it would be answered in a way that could not have been foreseen by any Greek. It is from this perspective, namely, the explication of the Christ event as an event for all peoples, that it becomes clear that the father of Jesus Christ has always been the one God from the very beginnings of Israel and, indeed, from the beginning of the world. There is a fundamental validity about the way in which the theology of the ancient church developed through the assimilation of the Greek spirit.

With these last sentences, I have already touched upon the next thesis.

THESIS 3: IN DISTINCTION FROM SPECIAL MANIFESTATIONS OF THE DEITY, THE HISTORICAL REVELATION IS OPEN TO ANYONE WHO HAS EYES TO SEE. IT HAS A UNIVERSAL CHARACTER

We are ordinarily urged to think of revelation as an occurrence that man cannot perceive with natural eyes and that is made known only through a secret mediation. The revelation, however, of the biblical God in his activity is no secret or mysterious happening. An understanding that puts revelation into contrast to, or even conflict with, natural knowledge is in danger of distorting the historical revelation into a gnostic knowledge of secrets.

In the Old Testament discussion about the self-vindication of Jahweh, it is his acts in history that were the events through which Jahweh proved his deity to all peoples, not just to

Israel.[10] What Jahweh accomplished in history cannot be written off as the imagination of the pious soul, for its inherent meaning of revealing the deity of Jahweh is impressed on everyone.

In this way Paul can say: "By the open statement of truth we would commend ourselves to every man's conscience in the sight of God" (II Cor. 4:2). H. Schulte has noted with justice that Paul is not sharing a secret knowledge after the manner of the gnostics. "The Gospel is no dialectic play between the state of revelation and hiddenness, but is fully revealed" (Schulte, *op. cit.*, p. 24). It is not without significance that Paul uses the philosophical term "conscience" in this passage.[11]

In a similar vein, Paul can speak of those who do not wish to see the truth that is manifest. The fact that some do not believe does not mean that the gospel is accessible to only a few, but that "the god of this world has blinded the minds of the unbelievers" (II Cor. 4:4) so that they cannot see the truth of the revelation of God in the fate of Jesus, a revelation that is available to all.[12] Nothing must mute the fact that all truth lies right before the eyes, and that its appropriation is a natural consequence of the facts. There is no need for any additional perfection of man as though he could not focus on the "supernatural" truth with his normal equipment for knowing. The event, which Paul witnessed, took place totally within the realm of that which is humanly visible. In particular, the Holy Spirit is not an additional condition without which the event of Christ could not be known as revelation. Bultmann has rightly insisted that Paul never describes faith as a gift of the Spirit, but rather that the Spirit is described as the gift received by means of faith,[13] in that which the gospel proclaims, which for its own part belongs to the sphere of the Spirit so long as it relates to the eschatological event. The paradox that there are persons who will not see this most evident truth does not absolve theology and proclamation from the task of stressing and showing the ordinary, and in no way supernatural, truth of God's revelation in the fate of Jesus. Theology has no reason or excuse to cheapen the character and value of a truth that is open to general reasonableness.

To say that the knowledge of revelation is not supernatural does not mean that man is only confirming what he already knows through the force of his own intellect. In this respect, no one comes to the knowledge of God by his own reason or strength. This is not only true about the knowledge of God, but about other experiences that we have. The divinely revealed events and the message that reports these events brings man to a knowledge he would not have by himself. And these events *do* have transforming power. When these are taken seriously for what they are, and in the historical context to which they belong, then they speak their own language, the language of facts. God has proved his deity in this language of facts. Naturally, these experiences are not to be treated as naked facts, but are to be seen in their traditio-historical context. If we are to take these facts seriously, nothing ought to be inserted so as to allow them to be seen in a way different from what would naturally emerge. That these and also other events are veiled from many men, indeed, from most men, does not mean that this truth is too high for them, so that their reason must be supplemented by other means of knowing. Rather, it means that they must use their reason in order to see correctly. If the problem is not thought of in this way, then the Christian truth is made into a truth for the in group, and the church becomes a gnostic community.

The history of Israel all the way to the resurrection is a series of very special events. Thus they communicate something that could not be gotten out of other events. The special aspect is the event itself, not the attitude with which one confronts the event. A person does not bring faith with him to the event as though faith were the basis for finding the revelation of God in the history of Israel and of Jesus Christ. Rather, it is through an open appropriation of these events that true faith is sparked.

This is not to say that faith is made superfluous by the knowledge of God's revelation in the events that demonstrate his deity. Faith has to do with the future. This is the essence of trust. Trust primarily directs itself toward the future, and the future justifies, or disappoints. Thus a person does not come to faith blindly, but by means of an event that can be appropriated as something that can be considered reliable. True faith is not a state of blissful gullibility. The prophets could call Israel to faith in Jahweh's promises and proclaim his prophecy because Israel had experienced the dependability of their God in the course of a long history. The Christian risks his trust, life, and future on the fact of God's having been revealed in the fate of Jesus. This presupposition must be as certain as possible to him. Otherwise who could expect to obtain a participation in the life that has been manifested in Jesus, if such a presupposition were not oriented to the future?

There is a consequence for the Christian proclamation from this point. The proclamation of Christ presents, for those who hear it, a fact (taken to be reasonably and reliably true) that in the fate of Jesus of Nazareth, God has been revealed to all men.[14] The proclamation of the gospel cannot assert that the facts are in doubt and that the leap of faith must be made in order to achieve certainty. If this sort of assertion were allowed to stand, then one would have to cease being a theologian and Christian. The proclamation must assert that the facts are reliable and that you can therefore place your faith, life, and future on them.

The knowledge of God's revelation in the history demonstrating his deity must also be the basis of faith. Faith does not need to worry that this knowledge has been altered because of shifts in historical research, just as long as this current image of the facts of history allows him to reassess and to participate in the events that are fundamental to it. This far-reaching independence of faith from the particular form of historical knowledge out of which it has come is founded on the fact that, in the act of trust, faith transcends its own picture of the event. The event has its own foundation in that it relies on the God who reveals himself in it. In the trusting surrender of his existence, the faithful man is thrust beyond his own theological formulations and open to new and better understandings of history, which are the basis for his life. It is through such faith that the patriarchs of Israel had a part in the fulfillment, in Jesus Christ of the promises given to them, a fulfillment very different from anything that they might have been able to imagine. Through such faith, men have a part in the same history of God even though their ideological formulations of the history of God are irreconcilable. Such men are not only reciprocally bound to each other through faithful participation in the one history, but are also bound to those men who have no understanding of what the two are arguing about. Nevertheless, only the knowledge of God's revelation can be the foundation of faith, no matter how confused or mixed with doubt such knowledge might be. It should also be emphasized that it is not knowledge, but the resulting faith in God that secures participation in salvation.[15]

To what extent is God manifest in the history of Israel and in Jesus of Nazareth? How does he prove his deity? The following theses will attempt to furnish answers to these questions.

THESIS 4: THE UNIVERSAL REVELATION OF THE DEITY OF GOD IS NOT YET REALIZED IN THE HISTORY OF ISRAEL, BUT FIRST IN THE FATE OF JESUS OF NAZARETH, INSOFAR AS THE END OF ALL EVENTS IS ANTICIPATED IN HIS FATE

In the history of Israel, Jahweh had not proved himself to be a God for all men. He had only established himself as the God of Israel. This came about in a way that is quite understandable, although it is hardly applicable to us as non-Israelites. Jahweh had proved himself to be a powerful God in the eyes of Israel by delivering the land promised to Israel. And as long as Israel remained in possession of the land, the knowledge of being under the protection of his might enabled Israel to acknowledge the one to whom it was obligated for such possession. This kind of thinking is clearly understandable, and only the greatest superficiality would ignore the evidence of this complex. It would be a superficiality of a type that would see all earthly developments as nothing but human arrangements and involvements. In any event, the occupancy of the land is not proof for us of the deity of Jahweh in its fullest sense, since we are heirs of the Greek philosophical tradition and can give the name God in an unqualified way only to the one God of all men, and can understand the gods of the religions as at best representations and analogies of the one God. From this point of view, to understand the deity of Jahweh in any other way would be to allow the divine figure of a religion to surpass the concept of God in philosophy. Israel's or Judah's faith in Jahweh was matured in crisis through the loss of the land in the destruction of the year 587. Only because the prophets had for a long time been sounding the warning about just such a catastrophe could it later be understood as the self-vindication of Jahweh. Thus, the faith of Israel survived the collapse of its own national identity and the temporary loss of the gifts of salvation and pointed to Jahweh's new proof of salvation. This understanding had been remarkably substantiated by the prophets through the course of events that had already been proclaimed.

In the times of Ezra and of the Maccabean revolt, when the new salvation was thought of as in the present, it still appeared as something strictly provisional.

Whenever the historical self-demonstration of Jahweh in his acts was viewed as being definitive and lasting, this demonstration still retained a provisional character. It is always surpassed with new events, new historical activity in which Jahweh presents himself in new ways. Thus, we saw that it is only the end of all events which could bring in the final self-manifestation of Jahweh, the perfection of his revelation.

Through an extraordinary vision the apocalyptic writer sees ahead to the end of all things. The historical plan of God was disclosed to him ahead of time. However, wasn't the apocalyptic view itself corrected by the further course of history? In contrast, the witness of the New Testament is that in the fate of Jesus Christ the end is not only seen ahead of time, but is experienced by means of a foretaste. For, in him, the resurrection of the dead has already taken place, though to all other men this is still something yet to be experienced.

If we allow the apocalyptic expectation of the end of the world to be linked with the general resurrection of the dead, then in these events the God of Israel has proved himself to be the one God of all men. More can be said about this in the context of the following thesis. Let us remember: The one and only God can be revealed in his deity, but only indirectly out of a totality of all events. This was also the lead thought regarding the true form of the divine in Greek philosophy. It is only that this philosophy did not understand the totality of reality as a history always open to the new contingency, but rather took it to be a world with unchangeable structures of order.[16] In this way, one could make inferences about the true form of the divine on the basis of the totality of phenomena that are known to every period of time. But, in the context of the history of thought, the Greek cosmos offered only a narrow conception of reality that was open to man's experience. The biblical experience of reality as history is more inclusive, since the contingency of the real event is included in this conception. Experience of the reality of history is superior to that connected with the contemplation of the cosmos. This is true both then and now because history can accept cosmic reflection as an element within it and make the regularity expressed in this cosmic reflection more realistic in structure and movement by providing it with a broader base of presuppositions. In such a situation, the God who is revealed out of the totality of history in this indirect way would also be the dominant answer to the philosophical question about God.[17]

Now the history of the whole is only visible when one stands at its end. Until then, the future always remains as something beyond calculation. And, only in the sense that the perfection of history has already been inaugurated in Jesus Christ is God finally and fully revealed in the fate of Jesus. With the resurrection of Jesus, the end of history has already occurred, although it does not strike us in this way. It is through the resurrection that the God of Israel has substantiated his deity in an ultimate way and is now manifest as the God of all men. It is only the eschatological character of the Christ event that establishes that there will be no further self-manifestation of God beyond this event. Thus, the end of the world will be on a cosmic scale what has already happened in Jesus. It is the eschatological character of the Christ event as the anticipation of the end of all things that alone can establish this development so that from now on the non-Jew can acknowledge the God of Israel as the one true God, the one whom Greek philosophy sought and the only one who could be acknowledged as the one true God from that time on. This is a point of view quite distinct from the self-vindication of Jahweh through the giving of the promised land to Israel. This acknowledgment, and the accompanying ratification of the universal revelation of God in the fate of Jesus, is itself a fact that became a part of world history through the absorption of the classical world into the ancient church.

In the fate of Jesus the God of Israel is revealed as the hidden God. The hiddenness and transcendence of the God who is revealed in the crucified Jesus surpassed the canon of the incomprehensibility of the philosophical concept of God. On the basis of the above-mentioned reasons, one can really know that the resurrection of the crucified one is the eschatological self-revelation of God. However, no one person can see everything or exhaust what is specifically contained in this self-manifestation of God. There are many concrete things that can be said about this, but at the same time there is an incomprehensible future that stands before us in the "then" and "there" of the Jesus event. We can speak of the resurrection, but we are not able to exhaust all the implications of what we say with that term, although what we appropriate from the event of the resurrection of Jesus, namely, our life's reality in the light of the final decision, does place us in a position to speak about the self-revelation of God and justifies such language even now. From the point of view of our comprehension, the inexhaustibility of the event of revelation as an eschatological event is very important. Otherwise one would easily misunderstand what has previously been said about the knowledge of the self-disclosure of God as a claim to knowing everything.

In the fate of Jesus, the God of Israel is revealed as the triune God. The event of revelation should not be separated from the being of God himself. The being of God does not belong just to the Father, but also to the Son. The Holy Spirit also shares in the being of God by virtue of his participation in the glory of God that comes to life in the eschatological congregation. Hegel and Barth are correct in the principle of grounding the doctrine of the Trinity in revelation. In all periods of history, one can experience with special force the incomprehensibility of God in that the dualism of the one and the many, which always guided Greek conceptualization of God, is here overcome. All of this is connected with the fact that the doctrine of the Trinity formulates the concept of God as a historically experienced revelation.

If the fate of Jesus Christ is the anticipation of the end, and thus the revelation of God, then no further revelation of God can happen. Of course, God is active even in the events after Christ, and he also discloses himself in that time, but not in any fundamentally new way, but rather as the one who has already been revealed in the fate of Jesus. This does not mean that nothing new happens after Christ. The history after Christ bears his mark. Its special motifs seem to become noticeable for the first time in the thrust that is contained in the Christ event. The history after Christ is determined in essence by the proclamation of the revelation in Christ. In the effects of this proclamation, new facts are created in the history of the world. I would mention only two at this point: the linking of the gospel with the Greek spirit and the assumption of responsibility of civil justice during the Constantinian period on the basis of an understanding of the eschatological congregation. The church is always tempted to play down the still-impending future of the eschatological life and to forget that all forms of Christian life in this world are provisional. This was also true of the Constantinian era, and the result of the church's forgetfulness had enormous consequences for the history of the world, including the anti-Christian turns in the subsequent Christian history. But even this has a part in the unity of history by means of its relation to the Christ event. To pursue all the particular connections would be the task of a theology of church history within the necessary framework of a theology of history. But no new self-disclosure of God would become evident in the extension of the eschatological Christ event in the subsequent history.

If one is careful to note the eschatological character of the fate of Jesus as the presupposition for the nature of God's revelation, then the thought structures that plagued the concept of the historical revelation of God in German idealism are avoided. (1) While it is only the whole history that demonstrates the deity of the one God, and this result can only be given at the end of all history, there is still one particular event that has absolute meaning as the revelation of God, namely, the Christ event, insofar as it anticipates the end of history. (2) So long as man is still under way toward the still-open future of the *eschaton*, the Christ event is not overtaken by any later event and remains superior to all other concepts as the anticipation of the end. Finally, (against Rothe) it satisfies the eschatological character of the Christ event to see in it the self-revelation of God. Without that understanding of the event, a supplementary kind of inspiration must be presupposed.

THESIS 5: THE CHRIST EVENT DOES NOT REVEAL THE DEITY OF THE GOD OF ISRAEL AS AN ISOLATED EVENT, BUT RATHER INSOFAR AS IT IS A PART OF THE HISTORY OF GOD WITH ISRAEL

The way of Jesus of Nazareth and the revelational meaning of his fate is first understood from the viewpoint of the history and traditions of Israel. The Father of Jesus Christ was the God of the Old Testament, the God of the prophets, and of the Law that Jesus interpreted. It is precisely the incomparably full authority of the interpretation of the Law by Jesus as well as his whole manner of action that is understandable only from the background of the Israelitic spirit, namely, as a special form of the proleptic unveiling of the eschatological event that the apocalyptic writers claimed for themselves (or their pseudonyms). This was a link between Jesus and the self-understanding of the prophets. The peculiarity of Jesus' consciousness of authority, which distinguished him from the apocalyptic writers, ought to be connected with his conviction of the immediate nearness of the end. However, this distinction must still be seen as having arisen out of the soil of prophetic and apocalyptic traditions. This conviction links Jesus also with John the Baptist. What distinguishes Jesus from John, and what makes his activity a claim exceeding John's, is that Jesus proclaimed the impending end, not just as a judgment calling for repentance, but in a manner that presented himself as the eschatological salvation. It is for this reason—quite apart from the Jewish presuppositions—that the question about his authority must be put to him with such urgency. As Ulrich Wilkens has shown, it is from this perspective that the journey of Jesus to Jerusalem and his conduct there is understandable. The appearance and the fate of Jesus is thus decisively defined by means of the prophetic-apocalyptic expectation of the end, no matter how much this is recast in the proclamation of the presence of salvation. This connection is even clearer, if that is possible, in the primitive Christian message about the resurrection of Jesus. The resurrection of Jesus first assumed the meaning of being the anticipation of the end in connection with the understanding of history in the apocalyptic literature. It was only within the horizon of the apocalyptic expectation that the disciples of Jesus would designate as "resurrection" all experiences of the Living One who is distinct from earthly life on the other side of death. In these experiences, the Jesus whom they trusted is again acknowledged. In the sphere of this expectation, the appearance of the risen Jesus had its own language. The resurrection of Jesus is not just the divine authentication of the pre-Easter claim of Jesus concerning an authority reaching beyond any earthly authority. It also means the end has broken in with the fate of Jesus and that God is manifest in him. The story of the conversion of Paul shows how in the horizon of the apocalyptic expectation the fact of the resurrection of Jesus has a ready-made eschatological meaning.[18] In the light of this it would be possible to connect, in a very particular way, the promises of Israel to the fate of Jesus, just as the primitive Christian proof from scripture has done.

If one sees the meaning of the Old Testament background, and in particular the apocalyptic expectation of the end, and its significance for the primitive Christian knowledge of the Christ event, he can understand the fundamental problem of the Christian mission to the Gentile. How can the fact of the revelation of God in the fate of Jesus be made understandable

to non-Jews who have no real part in the apocalyptic expectation of the end? For a Jew at the time of Jesus, everything else
can come out of the fact of the resurrection of Jesus. Thus, for
him everything would hang on the one question: Was Jesus
resurrected or not? Whoever is afraid of the consequences
must try to deny the facts. Thus, the resurrection of Jesus is
transmitted only by his disciples and those who have come to
faith in the confrontation with the Resurrected One. All of this
would be quite different for the non-Jew who would not bring
the Old Testament or the apocalyptic expectation to the
question. To the extent that the non-Jew had problems with
the Old Testament concept of God in its context of sovereign
freedom and with the truth of the apocalyptic expectation of
an end of the world with a general resurrection of the dead, to
that extent the non-Jew would also not be convinced about
the consequences associated with the resurrection of one man
from the dead, namely, that the fate of Jesus is the revelation of
the Israelitic God as the one true God. Experiences superficially
similar to the resurrection of Jesus, when taken out of its
historical context, are spoken of in Hellenistic times, about
prominent men. The distinction between the situation of the
Gentile and the Jew needs continually to be kept in mind.

The primitive Christian mission among the Gentiles made the
expectation of the end and the resurrection of the dead part of
its mission kerygma (I Thess. 1:9f.; Heb. 6:2), and for good
reason. Paul correctly saw that the presupposition of the mission
is the resurrection of Jesus (I Cor. 15:16). As Luke's presentation has it, the denial of this presupposition is also the denial
of the Pauline gospel as it is proclaimed in Athens (Acts 17:32).
How is its truth to be made understandable to the Gentile? The
answer that we have from this time in history is that of Justin
(Apol. I, 18, 6). He is satisfied with a reference to the omni-
potence of God. It is very difficult to assert from this, however,
that the reference was satisfying to others. Just as the Old
Testament conception of God had to confront Greek philosophy,

so also it was necessary for the apocalyptic expectation of the end to confront the philosophical conception of the immortality of the soul. However, at this point one has the impression that the issue was not correctly stated. In the history of theology the concept of immortality has largely overshadowed the hope for the resurrection, which pointed to a new being for the whole man.

Perhaps the knowledge of modern anthropology, which has assisted the critic of the philosophical thinking about immortality, could be of further help at this point. The anthropological insight into the indissoluble linkage of those phenomena that we are in the habit of dividing into body and soul makes impossible the conception of an isolated "soul" and its continued existence. This concept has no value. Still, it does have a meaningful function in the philosophical tradition. This can also be understood today out of anthropological presuppositions. The thought about the immortality of the soul was in fact an expression of the unending openness of man to go beyond any given situation, so that even death is not to be taken as a limit. The modern expression of this would be man's openness to the world by the very nature of his constitution. After this concept of the immortality of the soul has been disposed of in the critical process, the uniqueness of human existence still searches for a new expression or symbol. (The conception of an event that is beyond all experience cannot be anything but a symbol.) Now, when one considers that the definition of man, from this point of view as well as from others, must be the same for all men, then there is perhaps a new light on the truth of the apocalyptic expectation of one impending end event that is to be for all men.

THESIS 6: IN THE FORMULATION OF THE NON-JEWISH CONCEPTIONS OF REVELATION IN THE GENTILE CHRISTIAN CHURCH, THE UNIVERSALITY OF THE ESCHATOLOGICAL SELF-VINDICATION OF GOD IN THE FATE OF JESUS COMES TO ACTUAL EXPRESSION

The eschatological character of the revelation of Israel's God demanded the turn to the whole human community. Thus, in the same way the gospel to the Gentiles came to be seen as a necessary consequence of the eschatological character of the Christ event. It has already been mentioned that the proclamation in the Gentile world of the universal deity of the God of Israel could not bypass the philosophical question regarding the true form of the divine. This question and its postulate was already taken into service in the time of the early church's mission, as a criterion from which the universality of the God revealed in Jesus was proved. The gnostic thought about revelation appears to have played a role during the time of transition. It was the means by which the eschatological significance of the Christ event could be expressed. It functioned in this way where the apocalyptic presuppositions could no longer be understood. In actuality, it must often have been difficult to distinguish the eschatological presence of the new aeon inaugurated by Christ, in which the earliest Christians lived, from the pneumatic otherworldliness of the gnostic. Attestation of this difficulty can be found in the Corinthian correspondence of Paul. There, as well as previously, it was a question of the linkage of the experience of the end of the visible world, and a new reality, with the knowledge of the true God.

Already Paul had noted the deep-seated opposition between the proclamation of Christ and the gnostic redeemer myth. This opposition cannot be presented in its fullness here. It must suffice to make the assertion that the gnostic thinking about revelation (which can be expressed with the technical term φανεροῦν) stands opposed to the biblical understanding of revelation in many points:

1. For gnostic thought, revelation occurs as a direct communication, as an appearance of the heavenly pneuma through the revealer. Opposed to this is the biblical thought that is characterized by the element of indirect revelation on the basis of God's activity in history.

2. For gnostic thought, revelation is not directed to the mind, but surpasses the ability of the mind and turns itself to the Spirit or—in Christian gnosis—to faith that is understood in a way analogous to pneuma in gnosticism (Diogn. 8:5, 10:1, 11:2). In contrast, the revelation of the biblical God is demonstrated before all eyes for the benefit of all people. It is not a secret knowledge available to the few.

3. The gnostic understanding of revelation involves the appearance of the divine in the human. From this perspective, the interest of the gnostic-influenced theology concentrated on the incarnation. This is true even in the opposition to gnosis. This can be seen in the assertion made in opposition to gnosis that stressed that the revealer has truly entered into human existence and is identical with a specific human being. The opposition's dependence upon gnosticism can be seen in the concept of a direct revelation, which is gnostic in origin. In contrast, the biblical-historical understanding of revelation concentrated on the fate of Jesus, on his proclamation, cross, and resurrection, for in this fate God has established himself as God.

In spite of these serious contrasts, the Christian proclamation of the universality and finality of the revelation of God in the fate of Jesus Christ did find extensive expression in the gnostically oriented concept of revelation. As a matter of fact, Jesus Christ, as the one in whose fate God has manifested himself in a final way, is the revealer of the highest God of which gnosis

could speak, and also mediated a participation in a life that is
not of this world. As the eschatological revelation of God, he can
clearly be spoken of as "the Word, in whom God has broken
his silence," as indeed Ignatius does. Likewise, as the early
church's Christology did in the reconstruction of the gnostic
thought about revelation, Jesus could become the appearance
of the divine in the human. The secrecy of the gnostic process
of revelation in a world hostile to God can itself serve as an
expression for the indirectness of the eschatological revelation
of the God of Israel in the absurdity of the cross of Jesus. When
an understanding of revelation can be found in the New
Testament that shares the features of gnostic directness, it
ought not to be dismissed as a deviation from the Israelitic-
primitive Christian thinking about revelation. The assimilation
of gnosis by primitive Christian theology was a process that was
hardly noticed; yet it performed the function of making the
God who raised Jesus from the dead intelligible as God to the
Gentile as well as the Jew.

However, it ought not to be overlooked that the appropriation
of gnostic conceptions, which originally pointed to a direct
revelation, can be justified in a theological sense only from the
perspective of the historical vindication of the deity of God in
the fate of Jesus Christ. Even the theology of incarnation, which
clearly had its roots in the gnostic understanding about revelation, is not an independent base for theological reflection, but
is only understandable as an interpretation of the historical
self-vindication of God in the fate of Jesus of Nazareth—in his
earthly activity, his cross, and, decisively, in his resurrection.
In this sense, the concept of incarnation is irreplaceable. The
concept of incarnation expresses the *development* of the process
of God's revelation and its coming to fruition in the one man
Jesus of Nazareth. This is the development from the distant
majesty of God to his imminence that is revealed for all time
in the Christ event. The statement of the incarnation is a final
résumé of the God of Israel's history of revelation. One cannot

simply reverse the relationship and understand the concept of revelation on the basis of statements about incarnation. To observe the ambiguity produced by such a procedure, one has only to look at the speculative theology of Hegel and his followers, or at the monophysitic undercutting of the old Alexandrian Christology.

One final question is to be raised about the relationship of revelation and word. Is this relation exhausted because "Word of God" is a concept that is taken over from gnosticism as an interpretation of the event of revelation, as, for instance, Ignatius does? Against such a conclusion is the wide use of the phrase "Word of God" in the primitive Christian writings. But what does this phrase and its roots in the Old Testament have to do with revelation?

THESIS 7: THE WORD RELATES ITSELF TO REVELATION AS FORETELLING, FORTHTELLING, AND REPORT

The inclusive designation of revelation in history as "Word" of God in the gnostic understanding of a direct divine self-manifestation is not to be confused with God's manifold and many-pronged involvement in the concrete execution of the history of revelation by means of his authorized word.

History is not composed of raw or so-called brute facts. As the history of man, the history of revelation is always bound up with understanding, in hope and remembrance. The development of understanding is itself an event in history. In their fundamental givenness, these elements are not to be separated from history; history is also the history of the transmission of history. The natural events that are involved in the history of a people have no meaning apart from the connection with the traditions and expectations in which men live. The events of history speak their own language, the language of facts; however, this language is understandable only in the context of the traditions and the expectations in which the given events occur. We have an implication of this in the case of the resurrection of Jesus.

The biblical traditions are to be related to the same God who brings the events of history into being. Our question is: To what extent are the words, authorized by the God of Israel and Jesus of Nazareth, to be related to the history that he activates? The three words in the history of revelation that are used in connection with the functions of God do not exhaust this question. However, they take care of the most important aspects of the relation of word and revelation.

1. The Word of God as promise: Israel experienced the self-vindication of Jahweh in the given events of its history largely as a confirmation of words of promise or threat that are still in the future. Nevertheless, the prophetic word is the vehicle of proclamation and thus is not of itself the self-vindication of God. If it is to be found in visions and auditions, these were not understood as the direct self-disclosure of God. One gains a revelation of God's deity in seeing the way in which he fulfills promises. There is a circularity in this. The prophetic word precedes the act of history, and these acts are understandable as acts of Jahweh only because a statement coming in the name of Jahweh interprets them this way. Then, as deutero-Isaiah often stressed, "establishment" of it is needed before it becomes revelation. The word of the prophets that announces history is still continued in the proclamation of the apocalyptic literature and of Jesus about the nearness of the impending kingdom of God.

2. The Word of God as forthtelling: The Old Testament essay has already shown that the Israelite Law of God presupposed the knowledge of the deity of Jahweh and also his self-vindication as demonstrated. Law and commandment follow as a result of the divine self-vindication. They do not

themselves have the character of revelation. They could be this only insofar as the acts that established Jahweh's Law indirectly showed who he was, just as his other acts did. This usage was also continued in primitive Christianity in that it was not just the Old Testament Law, but also the declarations of Jesus that were characterized as the Word of God. The authority of Jesus as the bearer of the authority of God himself is thus already presupposed.

3. The Word of God as kerygma: Because the first two functions of the Word of God within the history that revealed God penetrated into primitive Christianity out of the usage of the Old Testament, a third function emerges for the first time in the New Testament. This is most significant. It is a question here of the word that comes from the eschatological revelation of God.

By far the preponderant meaning of the designation "Word of God" in the New Testament is the word of the apostolic proclamation. The message of the apostles is called the Word of God, because it is decisively set in motion (I Thess. 2:13) through the appearances of Jesus (Gal. 1:12, 15f.). This is not because of human effort, but because of God himself. This is really more properly understood as a report of the event in which God is revealed, as the report of the fate of Jesus. This can be seen in the genitive constructions like Word of the cross, Word of redemption, as well as in the parallel usage Word of God and gospel. The appropriate response to this event of the eschatological self-vindication of God is that of "reporting," and this can be so proclaimed in every language, culture, and situation as the decisive act of God's salvation. In this connection, an objective and detached chronological description of this event would not measure up to what is involved in "reporting." Thus, the apostolic word in the sense of report is also essentially proclamation.

The issuing of the kerygma, as the report of the revelation of God in the fate of Jesus, is itself an element in the accomplishment of the revelation event. The self-vindication of God before all men cannot be thought of apart from the universal notification. However, the kerygma is not by itself a revelatory speech by virtue of its formal characteristic, that is, as a challenge or call.[19] The kerygma is to be understood solely on the basis of its content, on the basis of the event that it reports and explicates. In this sense, the kerygma is not to be thought of as bringing something to the event. The events in which God demonstrates his deity are self-evident as they stand within the framework of their own history. It does not require any kind of inspired interpretation to make these events recognizable as revelation. R. Rothe's assertion of the need for an inspiration that would supplement the outer proclamation of the manifestation and make it into a recognizable manifestation of God is an assertion that misses the point. Equally false is the thesis that Ludwig Ihmels proposed in 1910 to the effect that the outer manifestation needed to be supplemented by what he termed a "revelatory word" (*Wortoffenbarung*). The word of the kerygma is not its own revelatory event in any isolated fashion, but is an aspect of the event of revelation in that it reports the eschatological event. It is this eschatological event that is the adequate self-vindication of God and that activates a universal proclamation through which it is also made explicit.

In addition, the proclamation of the church does not in this respect have the character of a special revelatory word. The sermon as an event by itself is not revelation, but the report of the revealing history and an explication of the language of fact, which is implicit in this history. And in this respect, the sermon as a report of this history does indeed break into every situation as call and consolation.

NOTES

1. H. W. Wolff, "Wissen um Gott bei Hosea als Urform von Theologie," in *Ev. Theol.*, vol. 12, 1952/53, pp. 533–54, esp. p. 553.
2. W. Zimmerli, *Erkenntnis Gottes nach dem Buche Ezechiel*, 1954. In this book, the whole Old Testament tradition of this concept is investigated.
3. On this see G. Kittel, *TWNT*, II, pp. 242–55, and H. Kittel, *Die Herrlichkeit Gottes*, 1934.
4. *TWNT*, II, p. 242.
5. G. Kittel, *op. cit.*, pp. 242ff., and also D. Rössler, *Gesetz und Geschichte*, 1960, p. 61, note 4.
6. *TWNT*, II, pp. 252f.
7. Rom. 8:17f., II Thess. 1:7, I Pet. 1:7f. and 11, Luke 2:32.
8. This is the apt characterization of Bultmann concerning the whole of the primitive Christian thought about the Spirit, *Theology of the New Testament*, vol. 1, pp. 42f., 155ff., 337f.
9. Compare A. Alt, "Die Deutung der Weltgeschichte im Alten Testament," *ZThK*, 56, 1959, pp. 129ff.
10. See Is. 25:7, 11, 17; 26:6; 28:22ff.; 29:16, 21; 30:8, 19, 26, etc.; 36:23; 39:22, 27f. Further, second Isaiah 41:20, 23; 45:36; 49:23. In Israel's prayers concerning the help of Jahweh, the thought of the self-vindication of Jahweh had an established place in the structure and is in juxtaposition to the request: I Kg. 8:60; II Kg. 19:19; Bar. 2:15–31; Prayer of Asarjas 21. This list could be extended into the New Testament.
11. See G. Bornkamm, "Glaube und Vernunft bei Paulus," in *Studien zu Antike und Urchristentum*, 1959, pp. 119–37, esp. 129ff. and the presentation, pp. 133ff., in the important text I Cor. 14:1–25. His point is that Paul employs the rational argumentation and insight in proclamation so that he can express, in an understandable way, the truly unique form and conceptual development of the gospel.
12. The relationship of the event of revelation to the sin of man cannot be developed here in the particulars. The man turned in on himself by sin is closed off from God and also from reality, although he is continually living from newly experienced "realities." Wherever he was forced to appropriate a new experience or a new item that does not fit into the customary scheme of his life and world, then there always emerges, in opposition to the tendency of his own persistent self-will, the unavoidable reality of the facts of the case (or event) that confronts him. The same is the case with the activity that reveals God. The proclamation of this ought to urge the hearer to take this event seriously in its undeniable reality.
13. R. Bultmann, *Theology of the New Testament*, vol. I, #37; see p. 329 on Gal. 3.
14. Of course, the correlation of revelation and salvation cannot be discussed in detail here, since we are primarily concerned with the fundamental structure of revelation. However, the fact of this connection is presupposed throughout the development of these theses. For the man who is disposed to an openness toward God, revelation in its deepest sense means salvation, fulfillment of his destiny and his very being. All discussion about concrete benefits of salvation is faithful to salvation only insofar as they share indirectly in the nearness of God, and mediate fellowship with the end of everything. The revelation of God truly speaks to the sinner only as long as there is a possibility of new

communion with God, which gives him the power to turn out of his closedness to himself to an openness to God. To this extent, the salvatory meaning of God's revelation is essentially linked with its proleptic character. The revelation of God at the end of all history in the judgment of the living and the dead means only damnation for the sinner who cannot repent. This is the end of his human destiny. The proleptic manifestation of the eschatological revelation of God has the character of a turn of events that was deliberately chosen. It is the character of the revelation that it brings about a still more real participation in salvation and in communion with God.

15. The connection between faith and knowledge (I am not speaking of understanding, but of knowledge in the comprehensive sense of insight) is so complicated that it cannot be presented here in all its aspects. Suffice it to say that there is an existential movement in which both are bound to each other in a variety of ways. The knowledge on which faith is grounded is the present result of a process of knowing that is always open-ended. Faith cannot stop the constant probing and investigation of its source. Thus, while faith is not brought into being by an external cause, verification of its sources strengthens it. Doubt questions the knowledge on which faith is grounded and also tempts faith itself. This temptation ought to become a stimulus to make faith deeper and more truly certain. Thus, faith assumes that the ongoing knowledge will not pull the rug out from under it, but will lead to results through which faith will have new insight into its own foundations. Thus, the process of knowledge in which faith firms up its foundation is normally held in process by faith that is marked by an assurance that anticipates the results of the process of understanding. This is not unusual, for all knowledge takes place in view of the anticipation of its results and receives its impulse from this, although the anticipated results that are to establish faith seem to have an undercurrent of an extremely self-critical testing. The Christian faith can indeed come through strengthened in the assurance that it can hold its ground in every critical test, even in those times when there is uncertainty about the validity of faith. But in such times faith can persevere in the anticipation that its truth will be established in a future and better insight. This tension between faith and knowledge cannot be covered up, or else the nerve of Christian existence is destroyed.

16. For the latter I refer to my essay in *ZKG*, 70. 1959, pp. 1–45: "Die Aufnahme des philosophischen Gottesbegriffs als dogmatisches Problem der frühchristlichen Theologie."

17. The assertion that the one God of all men and of all time is revealed in the fate of Jesus is not a philosophical reflection, but is rather one that must be constantly confirmed in the everyday experience of reality in each generation. And the philosophical formulation of the concept of reality will also be related to this. This confirmation of the biblical God's deity in the whole of the present experience of reality (not after the manner of Pietism, in the experience of the conscience) is something that is later. This presupposes the self-revelation of God in the event of Jesus and the confirmation of this in the church of earlier generations. However, when the one God of past times would be manifest to our world and generation, then his deity must be confirmed subsequently in this world and in the life experience of the men of our time. It is the concern of a dynamic proclamation that this confirmation does function in an enlightening way.

18. U. Wilkens, "Die Bekehrung des Paulus als religionsgeschichtliches Problem," *ZThK*, 1959, pp. 273–93.
19. In his debate with H. Schlier, U. Wilkens has shown that the Christian kerygma cannot be distinguished from the gnostic revelatory speech on the level of a formal analysis of the challenge or call. Rather, it is the content of the apostolic message that distinguishes it from the gnostic revelatory speech ("Kreuz und Wahrheit," in *KuD* 3, 1957, pp. 77–108, esp. pp. 97ff.).

V

The Problem of Revelation in the Concept of the Church

Trutz Rendtorff

1. The Concept of the Church as a Point of Theological Orientation

In recent theological study, the concept of the church is no longer an isolated, specific theme in dogmatics. It has instead assumed a pivotal role in historical and theological discussion. At the same time, the concept of the church assumes a key place in the theological conception of revelation as a *present* reality. Our essay will be concerned with the concept of the church in the context of an understanding of revelation, with special attention to the present connection of revelation and the concept of the church, as seen theologically.

Our time has witnessed a significant shift in the conception of the church, and we shall begin with a brief review of the special role that the concept of the church occupies in present discussion. It has been asserted that we have lived to see the "rediscovery of the Church," that the church "in our time has been again experienced as a reality."[1] Connected with this "rediscovery" of the church is the specific awareness that contemporary theology is doing something fundamentally new. This is interpreted in the context of the history of culture and theology in a way that exalts this renewal above the immediate historical context and declares that the only times that are comparable to these are the "classic" eras of Christendom, the original biblical witness, and the Reformation confession.[2]

This decisively new awareness was born within the horizons of historical experience, vague though its explanation might remain, and the connection between this self-consciousness and the concept of the church is quite apparent. For with this discussion of the concept of the church, the problematic nature of the concrete existence of the subject of theology and the content of faith is expressed. The definite emergence of the concept of the church in contemporary theology does not for that reason demonstrate in any way a greater concern for ecclesiology in the sense of technical dogmatics: The central place of the concept of the church draws our attention to the fact that here the problematic nature of concrete experience is connected with the concept of the church, which in general has replaced the concept of Christendom. At the same time it proves that the content of Christian existence in the world is the goal of the theological orientation within the horizons of history. The replacement of the concept of Christendom by that of the church points to the effort to tackle the various theological aspects of this orientation from the same starting point as the church doctrine of the saving presence of Christ. The intended unified theological expression takes place when the understanding of revelation becomes concrete in the concept of the church. The particular character of this tendency to have a thoroughly unified theological conception can be clarified in our development of the concept of the church.

The most important feature of the new discussion of the concept of the church is the stress placed on the *distinctiveness* (*Andersartigkeit*) of the church in relation to the world. The "church has been experienced again as the *other* reality, experienced as something fundamentally different from the groupings and social organizations that make up our world."[3] This accent on the basic otherness and uniqueness of the church (which is interpreted in the light of its distinctiveness from every other reality that can be experienced in the world) is the common basic conviction of dialectical theology.[4] Moreover, this accent also universally defines the theological discussion in our day. In this setting, it is important to note the reference to the otherness of the church is not usually employed in discussing anything specifically ecclesiological. Moreover, the assertion that the church as church is not amenable to natural or scientific understanding is ordinarily made in stereotyped phrases that deny the validity of sociological, psychological, or historical categories. This is done, however, without pursuing the implications of the insights thus attained. The idea of the otherness of the church should make it clear that its theological concept is determined fundamentally and from the outset by the understanding of revelation. The church appears as a revelatory reality, in a sense that does not first permit a proof of its distinctiveness within its own context.[5] In modern times, the most consistent precursor of the practice of deducing the concept of the church exclusively out of an understanding of revelation was Hegel,[6] who conceived of the church under the perspective of the completion of revelation of the Spirit in the community. In Hegel, however, we do not find a particular and emphatic application of this conception to the fundamental otherness of the church.

If the otherness of the church is established as the theologically decisive orientation for the concept of the church, then this understanding of revelation becomes concrete in the context of the church. Indeed, this comes about in the fundamental distinction between the factual, historical church, which people often characterize with the expression "Christendom," and the true church, called "the church of the word" or "the church of Jesus Christ." This distinction sharpens the basic contrast between the empirical church and the presence of Christ in his congregation, which then offers an incentive to develop some bridge between the two. This contrast appears to be constitutive for the theological approach in such a manner that the actual church does not offer anything for a theological understanding. In this connection, the rediscovery of the church is tantamount to the theological reformulation of the church. The rediscovery of the church here means her re-creation. This deliberate movement away from the empirical, historical church and the development of a theological understanding "from within" also has its precursors in German Idealism. In his fourth address on religion, Schleiermacher began his discussion of the church with the following: "Rather let us subject the whole idea of the church to a new consideration, reconstructing it from the center, unconcerned about how much has become fact and experience."[7] An understanding begun in this way is, at the same time, a sharp criticism of the church, even if not in great detail. The characteristic of this criticism is that it does not refer to definite, concrete historical problems, but to the mere existence of the church.[8] The verification of this assertion of the otherness of the church, at any rate, does not present any particular problem, since its truth cannot be questioned by confrontation with reality.

Thus, the unsettling of the church in the historical context of the present comes to a climax most sharply in its theological understanding. This can be observed most clearly in the theological and ecclesiastical development of the last fifteen years, when the theological starting point, hardly reflected upon, became binding while socio-ethical and church-sociological themes raised in this connection were ignored. Thus, the understanding of the church's otherness as it was formulated in the early phase of dialectic theology was long ago formalized into a static structural relationship, in which the contrast to the world appears as a theological datum, which establishes the basis for the renewed missionary and ethical return into the world in its many aspects. While the new concept of the church at first produced a theological assurance of faith in its uniqueness, men subsequently realized that it meant the theological abandonment of a unified understanding of the world. The only way in which this unity can still come to our attention is in the form of an ethical appeal to assume the task of creating it. Thus, the pressure today is to attain a new mediation, which cannot be produced on the basis of any principle of otherness, but which must bring its own theological foundation into question. Moreover, we do not start with the concept of revelation, which

underlies the conception of otherness; rather, in accordance
with our chosen viewpoint, we inquire more precisely into the
theological connection between the concept of the church and
the revelation of Christ. In particular, the real problematic is
to be seen in the conceptual formulation of just this relation.

2. THE DOGMATIC PROBLEM OF THE CONCEPT OF THE CHURCH

The consensus now is that the dogmatic content of a theological understanding of the concept of the church is to be
developed out of the linkage of Christology and ecclesiology.
The starting point for a definition of the relationship between
the theological concept and the historical reality of the church
is also to be sought in this context. A general and unqualified
discussion of the "historicity" of all reality with which one
often seeks to establish a synthesis in the concept of the church
only serves to hide the existing difficulties.

Let us try to clarify the situation by sharpening the
connection between the concept of the church and the Christ
event. K. L. Schmidt has set out the formula that "ecclesiology
is nothing other than Christology."[9] This theological conclusion
is widely acknowledged in the tradition and carried through
in a variety of ways. And the special point that is intended in
this formulation is developed not only by Barth, although he is
one who has done it with greatest consistency.[10] We are concerned with the substance of the theme, which comes to
expression in a formal sense in the distinctiveness of the church
and in a methodological sense in the anchoring of this concept
in the understanding of revelation. The explication of this
must therefore prove to be very important.

First of all, it has to be determined just what kind of weight
will be attached to a new understanding of this aspect of the
church. The essence of the church cannot be grasped by simply
looking at the church itself, but must be thought of theologically
in its unity and connection with the Christ event.[11] Thus, any

ecclesiological concept has the ground cut from under it if it takes as a starting point anything like the following opposites: visible and invisible, essence and appearance, institution and congregation, individual and community. In place of such expressions, which presuppose the church as a given fact and which then investigate its inner composition, the question arises about the conditions whereby the church is possible at all. In line with this question, the discussion would revolve around the connection of the church with the Christ event or, in a reverse way, with the presence of this event in the church. If the answer is not to be an appeal to the supernatural, it is clear that one has to proceed with a view to the historical connection of the church to the Christ event. The precise definition of this relationship of the church with Christ establishes the perspective of the discussion. This problem exists as a consequence of historical thinking as it is known in modern times, as is at once clear in any review of the profound development that has taken place in the tradition.

A brief characterization of this tradition would be as follows:[12] The pre-Reformation doctrine of the church was consolidated in large measure by reason of its opposition to Donatism. Its concern about the essence of the church was directly linked with the definition of its inner and outer unity. The struggle for the unity of the church clarified the connection of the Christian with saving revelation. This unity of the church would lose any kind of continuity if it were directly related to the situation of the Christian in the sequence of God's saving acts. Augustine solved this problem in his anti-Donatistic concept of the church. First, the division of people, which is a fact that is present in a hidden way, is relegated to the time of the future judgment. Then, the unity of the church of this age is guaranteed in the church's possession of salvation, particularly in office and sacrament, through which the salvatory work of Christ is carried on. The point of interest for us is that the church's connection with the Christ event (which can also be expressed:

praesentia Christi in Christi corpore, quod est ecclesia) never came under discussion as a problem in itself. In contrast, his ecclesiology was developed around the question of the manner in which this presence is to be concretely conceived and of how it ensures the possibility of participation in the salvation through the unity of the church. A new accent is introduced in the Reformation, as can be seen in capsule form in Article Seven of the Augsburg Confession: "quod una sancta ecclesia perpetuo mansura sit," or "that one holy Christian church will be and remain forever."[13] *The horizon* of the discussion is here shifted to the *unity of the church* in time and to what gave this connection permanence. The new factor in the discussion was the exclusive connection of the certainty of salvation with factors that guaranteed the unity of the church in its specifically theological sense. The dominant concern was on the *means* of giving participation in and the distribution of salvation. However, the efficacious presence of the saving work of Christ was assumed without question. The problem of how present-day faith is related to the Christ event centered on a correct definition of the ways of participation in salvation. In retrospect, it must be said that the *unity* of this connection of church and the Christ event was not questioned at the time and thus there was no discussion of the problem of its presence. To this extent, we can say that the ecclesiology of the Reformation was in line with that of the ancient church, at least as we look at it from a modern point of view. The question of the connection of the church with Christ is taken up in earnest for the first time in the historically oriented thinking of our contemporary situation. For this type of thinking, the *completion of the revelation of God* in a historical sense is of decisive importance. This radicalized the problem of the connection of Christ with his church, so that it made the reality of the present faith in its attachment to the Christ event more historically oriented than was previously possible. In this problematic (which acknowledges the connection of the present Christian existence as church and the Christ event to be a question involving history), we can see the roots of the question of the church as it is defined today. We can allude to Schleiermacher, who first put the problem systematically and in whose dogmatics the total life of the congregation for the first time was defined in a historically concrete way as having established the thoroughgoing theological connection between Jesus' original consciousness of God and his effect on the religious nature of man.[14] This is why Schleiermacher is celebrated in the nineteenth century as a "churchly" theologian. Also, in the Lutheran neo-orthodoxy that followed, whose theology presented itself as "books of the church," the decisive problem of the church was the "continuation" of the efficacy of Jesus from the point of view of historical connection. This necessitated a precise investigation of the facts, and as a result for the first time the weight of the historical aspect of the problem was finally felt, but only implicitly and initially.[15] With the exception of the discussion about the constitution of the church that developed in the struggle over union churches or confessional churches, the whole of the nineteenth century is oriented to the question of the church as the prime theme of theological endeavor. While the explication of the historical connection with Jesus was the nerve center of the discussion, this in no way determined the way the question of the church as history was to be expressed. However, on this point there is no reason for a departure from the nineteenth century.

In any event, it becomes clear that the undeniable insight into the historical character of the Christ event is a problem in itself, and the connection of the church with it does not necessarily follow in the establishment of the understanding of revelation. As a consequence of the historicity of revelation, the continuity of post-Christian history becomes more problematic. This resulted in a much more complex relation between the concepts of revelation and church. The material issues in the ecclesiological discussions in the last century and a half witness to this. Therefore it is even more important to keep clearly in mind the connection between this prevailing problem and the theological insight into the historical character of revelation. There must be no compromise on this point in the development of the discussion about the church.

If we again turn to the beginning of the present discussion after this sketch of the history of the problem of the concept of the church, then the polemic impulse should be distinguished in the situation at the beginning of the dialectic theology. After the crisis concerning historicism, the task of developing a connection between the church and Christ assumed subjectivistic or ethical dimensions. Troelsch, who was committed to the historical aspect in a most consistent way, could not speak plausibly about the theological content. The difficulty of maintaining the connection between the presence of the Christ event and the history after Christ was so great that it was often lost. This was due to the persistence of historical data on the one hand, and the persistence of religious subjectivism on the other. The assertion of the presence of God in the unmediated reality of the religious world also presented a menace to the Christian faith. The independence of a given religion as a fixed standpoint in an analysis of its psychological, ethical, or sociological structure had to be separated into components. The dominance of positivistic concepts of history and the corollary of individualism suggested a change of thought. The issue is whether dialectic theology took up the question of the *historical* connection of the church with Christ or came to a dead end by following the emphasis on differentiation.

3. The Relation of Revelation and Church in Dialectic Theology

The positive insight into the necessary connection of ecclesiology and Christology that was made in dialectic theology resulted primarily in an accent on the Christ event, so that world history and church history became meaningless because of the stress on the uniqueness of revelation. The actualization of revelation having its center of gravity in an accent on the sovereign character of revelation as event only gains meaning against a historical thinking and cannot be understood in isolation from it. To sharpen the issue one may say that the unity of the church with Christ was not demonstrated by any theological conception of historical continuity that might have contributed to the establishment of this unity. Rather, the oneness of the church with Christ was reduced to its factual and structural relationships. Thus it appears in the quoted formulations of K. L. Schmidt: "Ecclesiology is nothing other than Christology."[16] This sentence can be understood in a variety of ways.

In the nature of the case, by concentrating the concept of the church on the doctrine of Jesus Christ, certain themes in ecclesiology do recede into the background. The decisive question of the connection of Christ and the church cannot be resolved with the temporal and thematic coupling of ecclesiology and the doctrine of revelation. It would only remain obscured. It is a very limited view that would allow the unmediated presence of Christ to come into the discussion along with the concept of the church. The church represents the revelation of Christ as something happening in the present. From the ecclesiological point of view formal expressions are at stake, like: "The church is, because it is an event"; "The church is the event of assembly"[17]; Its essence consists in its being "the collected congregation"[18]; "The being of the church is event,"—the concreteness of the church is established in this, "that God's work . . . is event."[19] The question of the connection between Christ and the church is reduced to the presence of the church as the actualization of the Christ revelation.[20] But, in the strict sense, the church of history wins a place only by the presentation of the Christ event by means of a correspondence of a structure,[21] by carrying over the dogma of the divine-human nature of Jesus into the doctrine of the church. Without going into a more elaborate dogmatic discussion, we can maintain the following: While the concept of the church is now discussed in the light of historically oriented thinking, it has still not produced any new dimension to the problem of the history of the church after Christ. One would expect some linkage of this history with revelation, but instead, this history is generally thought of as a "reflex" of an actualized revelation in the present.[22]

All this notwithstanding, the opening claims about the "rediscovery" of the church and the central role that the concept of the church has for contemporary theology are not simply fantasy. The point is to carefully note the convergence of discussions on the concept of the church around the question of the relation between faith and the *world*. "World" and "history" are two elements that cannot basically define the concept of the "church," yet they are the "over and against" which in relation to the concept of the church illuminate the concrete life of the individual Christian. Without exaggerating too much, we can say that we have to do here with a clearly political and ethical concept of the church. The development of the theological aspects of the concept of the church in a correspondence with christological theses is matched by a concentration on the problems of the world. We have already referred to this. Now the theological connection has become clear in its concretization of the concept of the church as an entity in opposition to the world, which in turn emphasizes its task of realizing the Christ event. However, at the same time we must exercise some caution about difficulties that seemed to have emerged at this point.

The church or congregation that conceives of its task only in relation to the world will lose meaningful orientation within the worldly sphere if its historical reality has no significant meaning for revelation in the present. For, in the actualization of the Christ revelation, which would come about because of its own dynamics and above the sphere of history, we find that the concrete historical base of the present-day church is of no consequence. If the event aspect of revelation (as well as the history of the church) is no longer acknowledged in the general outlines of world history, then it can hardly avoid a certain tendency toward arbitrariness in its understanding of itself and the world. Nor can this difficulty be overcome by means of an earnest concern for obtaining exact information about reality and by then becoming involved in it. The real problem is the question of an understanding of revelation. The understanding of reality in a theological sense is in a way bound up with an understanding of the church. And it can be developed only with an adequate connection between church and Christ as historical factors. The fundamental decision hangs on whether one takes the historical quality seriously or sets it into the classification of "historicity."

In this connection, we find ourselves looking at theories that have been developed about the existentiality and historicity of man. In this complex, the concept of the church falls into the background because the connection of faith and Christ is bridged in the unveiling of the structure of personality. The church of the word has only an instrumental function, but is not itself a concrete historical reality with any historical relevance, because the existential and potent character of personality must not be endangered by any form of facticity. The church is "nothing which is present in any mundane way . . . the church of the pure gospel is strictly invisible . . . and cannot be located in the world."[23] In this striking formulation the understanding of the church is oriented to faith, so that the call of God in the word of the kerygma is exclusively directed to the subjectivity of the individual with an accompanying exclusion of any historical or factual mediation, which also means the exclusion of the "churchly." In like fashion, Bultmann insists that the call of God "can be comprehended only by the individual." The proclamation of the word is accomplished only "as it is a word directed to me, the concrete man in a concrete situation."[24] The agreement here is that the presence of the Christ revelation has an actuality and "eventfulness" in its unmediated force that surpasses anything historical. As Pannenberg has mentioned in an introductory way, the connection with the self-understanding of man, especially as it is found in Gogarten, pushed the universal meaning of revelation into focus by means of an understanding of the world oriented to personality that opens a fundamentally new dimension to the Christ event. However, this universality remains obscure if its explication is reduced to the confrontation of world and Christ in the inner "historicity" of man's self. The inner logic will then call for interpreting the church as pure "linguisticality" (or as the event "of coming to language"), and the universal aspect is developed in a new conception of the world as world so that revelation is limited in application to the possibility of a new hermeneutic. The presence of the event of revelation cannot be recognized as the history of the church. If the church is to be a means of revelation it is through its "invisibility," which is akin to the "invisibility of the innermost event of the world."[25] The unity of reality as world calls for a concept of the church that always remains fluctuating between history and historicity. "The church has no history as the body of Christ, but is an historical phenomenon; and to be in the church and to be in an historical fellowship are two different things, and the relationship between the two is a paradox."[26] The unity of the church with Christ can hardly be illuminating if it entails the loss of a theological approach to the factual church of history.

We shall conclude this discussion of the church in contemporary theology by a summary of the basic positions of importance. The traditional concept of church is exploded because the discussion proceeds along historical lines and is concerned with the problem of the present church in its relationship to revelation in Christ. Here lies the root of the new ecclesiology.

This is true even if the contemporary debate limits the historical connection of Christ and his church to an existential interpretation. The very close connection between ecclesiology and Christology stands in the fore thematically, over and against a purely ecclesiological view. The issue is: Can this view do justice to the church of history or does this church stand only in a problematic relation to it? Finally, the concept of the church in contemporary theology is oriented to the reality of the world with a view to qualifying this reality by means of historical revelation. This question was first stated in view of an exclusive difference between the church of revelation and the world. This led to difficulties that involved the whole complex. Such a situation calls for a return to the primary question: the connection between the church and revelation as history.

4. The Problem of Revelation in the History after Christ

The universality of the problem that we have worked with and that cannot be denied cannot conceal the difficulty that the theology of the church raises in view of its historical content. We will avoid the implications that this difficult point creates for the over-all situation of Christianity, although theology in its intellectual responsibility cannot be blind to the actual experiences of the church. The reason for the thorough reduction of the concept of the church to the actuality of the Christ event, and the consequent limiting of the church to a present supernatural event rests on the fact that theology no longer has access to a view of the Christ event as closed in a historical and theological meaning. Neither can it show how the revelatory event in its once-and-for-all character determines history after the time of Christ.

While the historicity of the revelation of Christ is affirmed in the various theological positions alluded to, it is obvious in ecclesiology that the essential element of the church's past is avoided in the modern "historical" understandings of the unmediated presence of Christ. If the event of revelation is directly associated with the present, then the concrete existence of the church, within the content of her history, can hardly be made clear theologically, for it is simply the place for receiving the revelation event. This relationship must not be thought of theologically, as though the relation between Christ and the church is between two separate entities whose relationship must again and again be renewed. The church is thus often understood in a foreshortened way as the present congregation, and history as the material in which this relationship occurs. What is demanded is critical reflection on the whole of the church's history in order to approach the problem of the connection between the church and the event of revelation. The theological explication of the unity of the church with Christ has as its subject nothing other than the history of the church.[27] This history is subject to normal historical investigations, for apart from this, theological results will not be forthcoming. Put in another way: The concept of the church must begin with the factual connection between history as it develops after Christ and the Christ event, so as to take seriously the relation of the church to Christ. The theology of the church cannot overlook a systematic treatment of church history. Such history does more than provide illustrative data for the construction of dogmatic concepts; rather, it must be admitted beforehand that the history of the church as such is the sought-after connection with past revelation. Consequently, theology does not have to construct a relationship. Rather, it gains access to a systematic understanding of the church if it allows the church to reveal itself as history, as a whole, in full awareness of its openness and preliminary character. In any case, one cannot forget that the totality of this history does not make sense apart from Christ.

This type of material calls for special attention. This concept of the church must take history as its text. This is, of course, done as a dogmatic task that emanates out of these considerations and meets head on the theological connection of the church with the history of Jesus. The theology of the church must also take seriously the particular difficulty that what is meant here by the church is not a purely phenomenal entity. Indeed, such a definition is mere abstraction. Rather, the theology of the church must deal with history as it is qualified by the event of revelation, as history itself demonstrates. It is also important not to isolate particular phenomena for study, such as the church as an institution or congregation, the office of the church, the sermon, or the question of the subjective appropriation of salvation. Particular definitions have nothing to do with the representation of the church that is the subject of theological reflection in the continuity of its history.[28] However, one would not be correct in attempting a history of faith alongside a factual history of the church, because such a treatment of the facts would obscure the point that the basis of the church lies exclusively in the Christ event and that its own history of the experience of salvation stands in a necessary correlation with the revelation that occurred once and for all. The question really ought to be put the other way, as in the statement: The understanding of the church calls for its being thought of in connection with the Christ event. This is a historical judgment, an unavoidable one, and is to be worked out theologically in this sense. Any purely church-historical consideration, even if it is of a strictly limited period of time and has its subject matter limited strictly to the church, would prove itself to be inadequate in a historical as well as theological way.[29] The necessity to conceive of the church in its relationship to the Christ event comes out of its own history. Moreover, this way of looking at history is in accord with reality. The question of just how completely the church can be considered the church of Jesus Christ cannot be decided in any other way, because the mere existence of the church, or more abstractly, its structures alone would tell us nothing. The transcendent character of the church resides in its historical relationship to revelation. The traditional distinction between the empirical church and the true church is clear when eschatologically understood and as a consequence drawn from the fact that it is the Christian church. To this extent, the early church was correct when it defended the unity of the church against being divided on the basis of an eschatological expectation. Equally incorrect is any contrasting of the church as known in history with the original foundation of the church in the sense of a normative concept of a revealed church or with the prototype of the church in primitive Christianity, or in the Reformation. The tension in the concept of the church has its basis in the indissoluble relation to Christ, and is a tension that rests upon the fact that the church is not grounded on its own foundation, but on an initial fact of history—the Christ event. Thus, the contingent character of the church is grounded in just this connection with Christ.

This orientation to the finality of revelation also brings out, for the first time, the positive aspect of the theological problem of the concept of the church. The movement back into the church's historical origin is the first decisive definition of the corporateness of the church. It is under such a presupposition that the theological formulation concerning the indissoluble anchoring of ecclesiology in Christology comes to its proper perspective. This is the correct conceptualization of historical continuity. Indeed, revelation is not given as an experience of immediateness, but is still transmitted to us through the channel of history. Thus, the participation in the history developing after Christ is not to be seen in knowledge or in faithful trust, but takes place in a comprehensive way as the history of the church, which can only be opened up by an understanding of revelation.

The eschatological orientation of the congregation discloses for the first time the universal aspect of the concept of the church by means of the anticipation of the perfection of history in the fate of Jesus. This also draws attention to the fact that the continuity of the church as history does not just unfold out of

imminent necessity, but always contains something totally new
and unpredictable. In framing the concept of the church, it is
not enough to have it oriented toward a constitutive expectation of the future, a future that is based on the Christ event, but
also to keep in mind the universality of the history that develops
after Christ on the basis of the eschatological character of
revelation. This is not a generalized timeless postulate, but
something that takes place concretely as an aspect of the unity
of the church. The theological content of the unity of history
manifest in Jesus, the end of history, could be defined as the
explanation of the unity of the church as it lives eschatologically
in its concrete existence, standing under the signs of its future
end. As already mentioned, the question of the unity of the
church is not just a history of importance all by itself, from
whose end point we take the orientation for our investigation,
allowing the close connection with the problem of revelation to
be acknowledged as a result of a historical consciousness. Rather,
it is in this history that the unity of the church comes to pass in
a concrete way and not just supernaturally in its eschatological
existence, as might seem plausible from the perspective of the
Christ event.

The question of the unity of the church at once involves a
view of the universality of history after Christ, so that the
problem of the relationship of the church to the world is to be
taken up under this perspective of universal history, not in a
speculative way, but thoroughly oriented to the historical
insights that see the discovery, affirmation, and development of
the unity of the church as a fact in world history. There is really
no factual support for the theological propensity toward con-
structing a structural relationship between the church and the
world. The decisive shift in respect to the unity of the church,
emerging as a result of the historical review into its meaning,
also needs to be expressed in its theological form. Since this
discussion has unfortunately only dealt with the initial explication of the concept of the church, we can only raise one point

for consideration. The history of post-Reformation times has made it increasingly clear that the eschatological qualification of history as it develops after Christ does not present us with a timeless image or any set of givens that are sociologically determined along one line. On the contrary, its historical character is a remarkable manifestation of the complexity of the problem of the unity of the churches. This dramatic turn in recent times could be most precisely and comprehensively defined on the basis of the relationship between the unity of the church and the unity of the world. In spite of all the difficulties that might arise, this new situation challenges the theological enterprise to be open to the contingent newness of the event rather than protecting some established position about the unity of the church. It must seek out the new dimensions of unity in the world that have resulted from the revolution in the relationship between the churches themselves and between the churches and the political community. It can also grasp, in a new way, the unity of history in connection with the eschato-logical character of revelation. Precisely because it can proceed only in close connection with the problem of revelation, a theology of the church must always take account of the world historical process.[30] The question concerning the qualification of modern history, through the eschatological event of revela-tion as a new disclosure of its universal character, must remain obscured if the decisive aspect of the church under discussion is its difference from the world. The same is true if the unity of history, which is not congruent with the present existence of the church, cannot be made relevant theologically speaking.

In this discussion of the unity of the church, we were inter-ested in the direction in which the relation of revelation and church remains constitutive for the history after Christ and still presents itself as thoroughly historical. Since we could not deal with the concept of the church by itself as a separate entity, these remarks necessarily remain fragmentary.

Faith, as hope and the expectation of the future of God, has its concrete existence in the reality of this church, which is conceived as the historical continuity with the revelation of salvation through Jesus Christ. In this sense, faith can also take the present church as the church of Jesus Christ.

NOTES

1. O. Weber, *Versammelte Gemeinde*, Neukirchen, 1949, p. 8. In a similar vein H. E. Weber, "Theologisches Verständnis der Kirche," *ThLZ*, 1948, p. 450; G. Wehrung, *Kirche nach evangelischem Verständnis*, Gütersloh, 1947, p. 7. Also in agreement are K. D. Schmidt and J. R. Nelson in *EKL*, II, pp. 624 and 634, and E. Kinder, *Der evangelische Glaube und die Kirche*, Berlin, 1958, pp. 11f. A. Fridrichsen maintains: "the discovery of the Church's role in early Christianity is the greatest event within exegetical science in our generation" (cited by A. Nygren, *Christ and His Church*, p. 17. Also compare F. M. Braun, *Neues Licht auf die Kirche*, Köln, 1946. Ernst Wolf has asked if the new understanding of the church may be a fulfillment of A. F. C. Vilmar's prophecy that the doctrine of the church will be experienced for the first time in our days, *Barmen-München*, 1957, p. 129.
2. See, for example, H. E. Weber, *loc. cit.* "We have been made ready for the outbreak of this crisis for a long time, and in it we have been given a new breakthrough to the gospel of judging grace. . . . It was a promising beginning which brought into theology a new understanding of the reality of the church," and took up the task of "opening up the biblical witness to the service of the word of the present by means of the key provided in the Reformation confession" (pp. 450f.). One could further observe the characteristic expressions of the time after 1933: "What we are experiencing is nothing less than the new breakthrough of the reformation. . . . This Christendom from which we have come has been broken and consumed in the fiery ardor of God" (cited in K. Kupisch, Dahlem, 1934, *Ev. Theol.*, 1959, p. 500).
3. O. Weber, *op. cit.*, p. 8.
4. See, for example, E. Thurneysen, *Christus und die Kirche*, *ZZ*, 8, 1930, pp. 177ff., esp. pp. 181f.
5. Thus see E. Wolf, *op. cit.*, p. 11: "The question of the revelatory conception of the church is one involving the Church of Faith (*die Kirche des Glaubens*)" (125); cf. E. Kinder, *op. cit.*, p. 11.
6. *Vorlesungen über die Philosophie der Religion*, II, pp. 191ff. and 308ff. Cited in the edition of his works by H. Glockner, in vol. 16.
7. *On Religion* (Torchbooks, 1959), p. 148.
8. This is done in sharpest terms in K. Barth's *Das Wort Gottes und die Theologie*, *Ges. Vorträge*, I, München, 1925, pp. 64ff., and especially in his *The Epistle to the Romans*, pp. 330ff.
9. *TWNT*, III, p. 515.
10. *Ch. Dog.*, pp. 34, 45, 53, etc.

11. E. Kinder thus speaks of "indirect ecclesiology," *op. cit.*, p. 18.

12. See R. Seeberg, *Studien zur Geschichte des Begriffs der Kirche*, Erlangen, 1885; and E. Altendorf, *Einheit und Heiligkeit der Kirche*, or *Arbeiten zur Kirchengeschichte*, 20, Berlin, 1922.

13. (Translator's) English text cited from *The Book of Concord*, Tappert (ed.), p. 32.

14. *The Christian Faith*, #3–14, esp. #13.

15. See A. F. C. Vilmar, *Dogmatik* II, Gütersloh, 1874, pp. 186, 203ff., and *Theologie der Tatsachen*, Marburg, 1857, pp. 50ff.

16. Thus in Wehrung, *op. cit.*, p. 34; H. E. Weber, *op. cit.*, p. 459; O. Weber, *op. cit.*, p. 10; D. Bonhoeffer, *The Communion of Saints* (Harper & Row), in the formula "Christ existing as congregation," as developed in K. Barth, *Ch. Dog.*, IV, #62, 67, and 72. The dogmatic discussion in this essay is limited to one aspect of the problem without an attempt to do full justice to the precise intentions of the authors.

17. K. Barth, "Die lebendige Gemeinde und die freie Gnade," *Theol. Ex.*, NF 9, 1947, pp. 3 passim.

18. O. Weber, *op. cit.*; and also Thurneysen, *op. cit.*, esp. p. 202, speaks of the decisive act being that of "the coming together."

19. K. Barth, *op. cit.*, p. 5, cf. *Ch. Dog.*, IV/1, pp. 651.

20. Something like the formula of the "Lord who proclaims himself."

21. Cf. Barth, *Ch. Dog.*, IV/3, pp. 724ff.

22. There is a very thoughtful discussion of this problem of the history of the church after Christ by G. Gloege in *ThLZ*, 85, 1960, pp. 161ff.

23. F. Gogarten, *Der Mensch zwischen Gott und Welt*, 2nd ed., 1956, pp. 311.

24. R. Bultmann, in a discussion with C. H. Dodd's attempt to define the problem of history from the perspective of the concept of the church. Dodd, "The Bible Today," in *The Background of the New Testament*, Cambridge, 1956, p. 407.

25. F. Gogarten, *op. cit.*, p. 316.

26. Bultmann, *op. cit.*, p. 408.

27. In this sense, I agree with E. Kinder, who speaks of the church as "the new corporate life which emanates from the mission and work of Jesus Christ among mankind, and through which, the activity of salvation is carried out." *Op. cit.*, p. 15.

28. With such a statement, the possibility of relating the particular factors is not excluded. This is excellently done by C. H. Ratchow in *Der angefochtene Glaube*, Gütersloh, 1957, pp. 165ff., who takes up the relationship of scripture, office, and confession in a way that always remains open to the totality of the history of the church.

29. This can be seen in the unsatisfactory aspects of Troeltsch's study, which otherwise is a very comprehensive work. See E. Troeltsch, *The Social Teaching of the Christian Churches* (Macmillan).

30. Barth did this in a comprehensive manner in the third section of his ecclesiological discussion, esp. in "The People of God in the World Event," IV/3, #72, 1; still, this was remarkably unattached to historical correlation. See in opposition IV/3, pp. 18ff.